Dearest Carolyn,

Thank you for all the beautiful and inspired energy you brought to this book! And for just being YOU☺!

In Loving Friendship,

Cathrine Ghode

xox ♡

Journey of the Heart

An Anthology of Spiritual Poetry by Women

Catherine Ghosh

BALBOA.
PRESS

A DIVISION OF HAY HOUSE

Balboa Press books may be ordered through booksellers or by contacting:

Balboa Press
A Division of Hay House
1663 Liberty Drive
Bloomington, IN 47403
www.balboapress.com
1 (877) 407-4847

Because of the dynamic nature of the Internet, any web addresses or links contained in this book may have changed since publication and may no longer be valid. The views expressed in this work are solely those of the author and do not necessarily reflect the views of the publisher, and the publisher hereby disclaims any responsibility for them.

The author of this book does not dispense medical advice or prescribe the use of any technique as a form of treatment for physical, emotional, or medical problems without the advice of a physician, either directly or indirectly. The intent of the author is only to offer information of a general nature to help you in your quest for emotional and spiritual well-being. In the event you use any of the information in this book for yourself, which is your constitutional right, the author and the publisher assume no responsibility for your actions.

Any people depicted in stock imagery provided by Thinkstock are models, and such images are being used for illustrative purposes only.
Certain stock imagery © Thinkstock.

Printed in the United States of America.

ISBN: 978-1-4525-1782-7 (sc)
ISBN: 978-1-4525-1783-4 (e)

Balboa Press rev. date: 07/10/2014

I dedicate this book to my dear mother
for having joyfully introduced me to poetry
at a very young age.

I also dedicate this book to the extraordinary women
whose brave and beautiful voices appear on its pages,
with much gratitude for entrusting me
to unveil—through their poetry—
the timeless wisdom
all women hold in their hearts.

And I dedicate this book to you, the reader.
May it inspire your own voice to soar!

⁓

I lovingly offer this book to The Supreme Goddess
of loving devotion in the Bhakti Yoga tradition, Srimati Radharani,
Sri Krishna's dearest beloved.

"Poetry is a river; many voices travel in it; poem after poem moves along in the exciting crests and falls of the river waves. None is timeless; each arrives in an historical context; almost everything, in the end, passes. But the desire to make a poem, and the world's willingness to receive it—indeed the world's *need* of it— these never pass."

Mary Oliver

Contents

*The idea is to write it so that people hear it and
it slides through the brain and goes straight to the heart.*

Maya Angelou

Foreword

This beautiful book of verses speaks of the longings of the heart, of the habits of the mind, of the prayers often unspoken, silent cries in the dark to God, to the universe, to life itself—anyone who may listen and be moved. It is an ode to the muzzled yearnings of half of humanity. It gives voice to the voiceless, love to the unseen, opens up numinous possibilities for those seeking exodus from a shadow world of servitude and silence. At a time when female slavery is returning and trafficking in women is now counted in the millions, this poetic offering is at once a balm for the bent but unbroken sprit that is "woman" and a prophetic voice calling out to the men who can still listen and hear the truth.

Catherine Ghosh's folding of the poems into a thematic schema, her deft touches of prose about the meanings and messages of themes such as Muses, Nature, Light, Darkness, Transformation, Relationships and more, lends coherence and structure to the volume and thereby enhances the interpretive experience.

The explanations of the creative processes expressed by the poetesses are fascinating glimpses into the flow of inspiration that leads to the gift of a poem which, through human history, was the soul of song, the rhythm of fiery epics, the secret enchantment between the lover and the beloved—human and divine.

I have lived a life immersed intellectually, emotionally, and spiritually in the river of light that is the spiritual vision of Mahadevi, Shakti the Power of Reality, the only ancient theology of "God the Mother" that is still extant. Over centuries, Her faithful sons and daughters have written many songs to Her. They are a mixture of delight and disillusion, the thirst for liberation and the taste of freedom, of pain and bliss. In other words, they render reality as it is. The Mother is the Creator, Creativity, and the Creation. She is the blood and the beauty of infinite. Many of the poems in this volume also render eloquently the dual nature of lived experience; of the interwoven nature of loss and gain, of the muddy/messy, magical/mystical mixture that is life. They move the reader towards a deeper and more honest awareness of embodied reality. The poets of the ancient Shakti tradition would silently applaud!

Catherine Ghosh, in creating this remarkable collection, has gifted us all with a beautiful and poignant offering of the diversity and plenitude of women's voices. *Journey of the Heart: An Anthology of Spiritual Poetry by Women* is an important work that needs to be taken seriously, and experienced deeply.

Rita D. Sherma, Ph.D.
The Swami Vivekananda Visiting Professor
University of Southern California
June, 21, 2014

Sisters: talk to each other,
be connected and informed,
form women's circles,
share your stories,
work together,
and take risks.
Together we are invincible.

Isabel Allende

Introduction

If there were maps that could trace the journeys of human hearts, they would undoubtedly take the form of poetry. For poetry spills from our souls unabashedly, in word-rivers, that float our pleasures and pains upon them. Poems are like boats returning from wild seas, delivering treasures from their depths. We set sail for uncharted regions of existence every time we surrender to penning a poem. When we write poems, we draw lines between our hearts and our voice, becoming cartographers of our heart's lively shoreline.

We have reached a time in the evolution of humankind in which the voyages taken into women's hearts have become especially relevant. For the hearts of women hold within them deep spiritual insights, which after generations of being obscured, are now beginning to rise on the horizon—like stars in the night sky—guiding humankind through stormy seas. The following pages are filled with the discoveries that emerged from such expeditions, as women from all over the world and belonging to diverse traditions, explore the oceanic depths of their own beings through the writing and sharing of poems.

In my own life, I've often turned to writing poetry when no other means of expression seemed adequate to communicate everything that stirred within me. Poetry seems to have gigantic perimeters that swell like a universe and promise to contain as much of me as possible. This can be simultaneously alluring and terrifying, as part of me aches to bare my soul, while the other part shields me under a veil of silence. After centuries of having the female voice eclipsed, this inner conflict between withholding and releasing our voices is a common one among women. Yet living with the dichotomy can become an avenue to deeper self-awareness, as we habituate ourselves to honoring and expressing what stirs in our souls.

During the course of a woman's life, her relationship with her own voice will naturally go though many transformations. As a reflection of her state of being, a woman's words carry with them the power to change her experience of herself. Words can uplift us or deflate us. Like the moon's phases, our voices will wax and wane, appear and disappear across the ever-changing landscapes of our lives, as we cultivate an awareness of our own inner beauty, power and wisdom. For only a thin thread connects the confidence we invest in our voices, with the value we give ourselves. In exercising our individual expressive energy through composing poetry, independently of evaluating the literary quality of the poems themselves, we honor the collective, feminine voice worldwide, as it finds its strength more and more.

Yet, strength had nothing to do with the birthing of this project, which emerged most spontaneously from a moment of weakness in which my own voice was feeling very blocked. Frustrated in my own exasperated attempts to express myself, I gave up two magazine columns due to having missed publishing deadlines. What was inhibiting the release of my voice? On a quest to answer that question, I started a poetry blog online hoping to catalyze for other women what I hadn't achieved for myself: the fearless expression of words. It was within this irony that the voices of many women reached new shores.

In the following year and a half, The Journey of The Heart poetry blog became a welcoming space in which women could explore the power in their own words with the confidence that no one would judge them, rush them, or reject them. Emphasizing substance over form, the spirit of the project took off, and, as if by magic, the blog drew in exceptional women who effortlessly built trustworthy bridges between their words, their hearts, and each other. United though poetry, the women's voices naturally echoed one another's songs, despite their diverse theological, cultural and geographic origins. Like syncopated heartbeats in a choir, a universal rhythm began to drum though the women's voices, infusing their dialogue with unmistakable sacredness.

We experience the sacred anytime we feel ourselves as being linked to, or a part of, Divinity. A soothing sense of interconnectedness overwhelms us, as we savor the sensation of being one in substance with all of existence. The women who participated in this project cultivated this sacred connection with each other, the world around them and within them, through the transporting and unifying power of their poems. Their writings became vehicles into their spiritual cores, igniting the hearts of others as they emerged. Confident that a singular poem can hold within it the potential to reveal our most authentic selves, the poets unveiled their souls in vulnerable outpourings of words that inspired others to do the same, exploring their own divine natures in the process.

The poems trickled in at first and then arrived in waves, sometimes in accordance with the moon's phases. They drew from universal themes and archetypes that threaded them together like a garland of flowers while also celebrating their unique individuality. From enchanting muses to sources of light, darkness to dramatic transformations, the themes of the women's poems traverse the breadth of the feminine psyche, embracing everything that life sets before them, and within them, as part of their spiritual journeys. With relationships as their focus, poems began pouring in that spoke of intimacy with the Divine, with oneself, with one's sisters and beloveds. But most of the poems spoke about very active and fulfilling relationships with nature, in which we hear the women entering into dialogues with trees, the moon, the ocean, storms and other elements that reflect the wilderness growing wildly in their own hearts.

Appropriately, most of the oldest recorded poetry composed by women also reflects a heightened sensitivity to the natural world around us. From the ancient African Griottes—poets belonging to a long oral tradition of empowering women—to the ancient Sanskrit verses spoken by the Vraja Gopikas, our female ancestors strongly identified with Mother Earth. The contemporary voices that fill this book resound with the same message: every time we dishonor nature, we dishonor feminine energy. In being receptive to the voices of women, humankind gains valuable insights into life. As we face the dangerous consequences resulting from the mistreatment of women, and of our planet, we are beginning to see a resurgence of the feminine voice. It is to this new dawn in which women's voices thrive, that this poetry project pays tribute, with a vision toward restoring sacredness, in a peaceful harmonizing between genders and between species, in a world where women's voices are celebrated.

It is I, your muse,
hear me sing
Melodies of the moment
A breath of air in the spring.

Vrinda Aguilera

1

Muses

The fickle forces of creative inspiration have always intrigued me. They seem to come and go as they please without warning, and mischievously possess you when you least expect it. Always demanding one's full attention, muses seem to tease and toy with us until we yield to their power, and then, madden us with their sudden exits. Who are these muses, anyway? Do they come from within us, or from outside of us? Or is poetic inspiration the fruitful mingling of the two?

Many ancient cultures paint colorful descriptions of beautiful creatures descending from other realms to seduce us into poetic composition, like the Roman goddess, Minerva, the Greek goddess, Polyhymnia, and the Hindu goddess, Sarasvati. These celestial muses were not only believed to be the deliverers of poems but of wisdom and music as well, for poems were once melodiously recited and highly valued for the divine insights that flowed though them.

The poet, born with extrasensory perception, was chosen to serve as a yielding instrument in the hands of the gods. Yet it was considered both a privilege and a curse to be the receptacle of forces that created such mesmerizing beauty. For poets often lost themselves to their creative process, which both consumed them and exposed them in the most vulnerable ways. Being seen as such vessels of divine expression gave poets incredible artistic freedom to create without inhibitions, for great art flows independently of limits and judgments. Poets were the "makers" of such art, as the Greek origin of the word indicates.

To me, there is nothing more fascinating than listening to a poet describing their creative process! Tracing the exact origin of a poem is often laced with as much mystery as is tracing the origins of the cosmos. Where a poem comes from, and how it begins, is a secret that weaves beautifully elusive threads between the poet and the poetry.

In this chapter you will encounter poems in which women attempt to give words to this process: how they experience the making of a poem. The women describe poetry in colorful paradoxes: as angelic and wicked, familiar and foreign. They offer us metaphors to illuminate the feeling of birthing a poem from the fluttering of leaves in autumn to explosions of blossoms in one's heart.

Here poetry is equated with painting, bleeding, shining and dancing, emerging with both agony and thrill, and drawing liberating trails of both pleasure and pain. And although each process is as unique as the poets themselves, they all give the sense that there is something undeniably mystical that happens in the making of a poem: something which, unlike the characterizations of the past, feels very much like descending grace, dialoguing with divinity, even existential satisfaction. As many of these poems draw delightful parallels between the irresistibility of writing a poem and the very flow of life itself.

Oh, Poetry!
by Vrinda Aguilera

Writing poetry is a mystical process for me. When I fully surrender myself unto it, I find myself immersed in a creative process that engages my entire being- my mind, body, and spirit. The mystery of this practice is that while a poem may come from me, it is also simultaneously independent of me. There is an unknown, otherworldly aspect that also lends and injects itself into this dance with words.

I sometimes experience this creative energy as a mysterious personality who has many different moods and faces, who sweeps me away on adventures and transformational journeys. She, for I have given her a feminine persona, takes on the essence of whatever it is I need. Thus, she is powerful, comforting, seductive, graceful, and so much more.

How variegated is the wide range that can be found in the human experience- from the agonizing depths of deep despair to the dizzying high of great heights, and everything in between. It is precisely this ability to suffer and enjoy in so many unique ways that makes us who we are- spiritual beings having human experiences.

As a practitioner of *bhakti* yoga, devotional loving service to the Supreme, developing and cultivating personal, loving, relationships are the ends as well as the means to reaching the highest platform of love of God. For me, poetry is a means to such an end.

Oh, poetry- you capture my heart and stir my soul.

Oh, Poetry!

Oh, poetry, you thing of beauty.
Waiting in the shadows,
Your formless face veiled.
Humbly, patiently kneeling in servitude.
A gentle and chaste handmaiden
Cloaked and enshrouded in gauzy robes of ether

Oh, Poetry! You wicked seductress.
Shape shifting mistress of dusk, dawn
And the unclaimed spaces in between.
With your wild, untamed tresses
Your flashing glances smolder and burn.
You are insatiable, greedy
Ravaging and consuming me
With your relentless needs and demands.

You, my poetry! You're a graceful dancer.
Flowing, dipping, twirling, whirling
Mesmerizing your partner and audience alike.
Glimpses of milky white shoulders, delicate arched neck
Your movements are hypnotic and enchanting.
Such is your magic, your spell
That each think they, alone, sway in your embrace.

Poetry! You are a swollen ocean wave,
An embodiment of nature's power.
The force and strength of 1000 barreling freight trains,
Unstoppable and indiscriminate in your destruction.
Your white, foam-flecked peaks
Like the frothy beard of a rabid dog.
At times I have been caught in your swell,
Tossed about helplessly like a rag doll.
Half drowned yet half alive.

Poetry. You are a mother to me,
I, a newborn babe cradled in your arms.
Holding me close to your ample, comforting bosom
You smell faintly of milk and roses.
Gently shush shushing,
I am lulled into a state of drowsy contentment
As we rock in a worn cushioned chair
Back and forth, back and forth,

At times, poetry, you are like a razor sharp dagger
Lethal, unsheathed and without a scabbard
If I grasp you roughly,
You pierce and slice.
Leaving your signature, an angry, red sear.
'Handle with care,' is what you tell me
If I wish to use your pointed tip as a surgeon's tool,
Lancing the toxic boils that poison and pollute my soul.

Sometimes I cannot find you, poetry.
Alone and wistful I am left wondering,
Have you forsaken me?
Then, there you are!
Peeking mischievously out from around the corners of my words
Playfully, you have been hiding
You throw your head back and laugh in mirth.
My friend. We hold hands and run off to play.

Poetry, you are my angel.
You float down on soundless wings.
I cannot look at you directly when you are like this
You are suffused with and emanate a radiant, blinding light.
You help me forget everything else
And become one with my prayers.
A divine messenger, you carry my love to my Divine Beloved.
Tunneling through passageways hidden in the innermost recesses of
    my heart.
Salty tears seep out of the corners of my eyes in gratitude,
I hide my face in shyness.

Grace

by Edith Lazenby

Grace is the ultimate teacher for if we open to grace she always gives and shares and lights the way. Writing is my way of invoking grace, my way of knocking on the doors I cannot open without the beckoning of the Muse.

My Muse is not a person or place or thing. My Muse is Poetry; it is *the process*, for therein I reach to see what I might find. Reaching in gives me what I need to reach out, to have something to share, to offer what grace gives me as I continue to learn.

I have had many teachers over my life, people who have made a difference, shown me how to open my heart and mind in different ways. My teacher inspired this poem. She says she always finds feathers. Hence, I planted one here for her.

Grace

I read moments as if
Meaning a combination
To unlock the giving,

And the giving is grace
Unwrapping my heart so tears
Fall with sadness
And joy that all I know is
A sheath of being with words
That do what I cannot; paint
What I dare not see.
An eagle's feather
Lands at your feet.
Wings dance without bodies.
Music flies and flight
Happens after the body stops.
Need stamps its feet.
Fear locks the doors.
Anger boils and burns.
Yet when I move past that
I find in space what nature
Teaches: beginnings and endings
As forms, points
To start at or leave from.
In this calm
A snowflake
From God's mouth enters wind
And cold gives reason for warmth,
As time never knows self
In the way we think we do.

It Is The Inner Feeling

by Andreja Cepus

My poems were born through deep inner moments of experiencing my soul truth. And as soon as the words come out I feel this is a creation set free!

My poems are not freshly written. They come from a point in time, when my poetry cycle was, as I felt, completed and ready, perhaps, to be published in a book one day. To envision this, I had to embody all that came out from my soul in feelings and words. And, also, in my every day life, I sought to embody what my poems expressed.

The journey was long and not easy at all. But today, I as I am reading my poems, I see how much my Soul knew what she was writing about and how I had a chance to go through these experiences to fully embody my poems.

I see my poems as a type of universal truth that speaks to your heart without the use of many words. In that light, I am now ready to share my poetry, in hopes that you see the story of the potential in just one heart to invoke the flame of purity and love in every one who feels the poems. This poem was born in one of such deep moments.

It Is The Inner Feeling

It is the inner feeling
Innermost deep answer
Emerging from the very core of being
It is the source
Of a new me
Laboring my new self
In the quiet moments of day
A lonely feeling of fear
Is fading away
When inner knowingness prevails
And I surrender to Life.
No one can know,
It is just me facing myself
In the quiet moments of day
With a heart full of grace.

The Thrill of Creating

by Naomi Stone

I love to write in the very early morning before dawn. I feel that at this time creativity is so heightened: aligned and attuned with a greater Light and Love. In my early morning writings I celebrate the Beloved. I think once we connect on a deeper level with God as a Beloved, the mystic in us has to take over, because God is more than we could ever know: always creating and relating according to our open hearts and surrendered wills.

Sometimes I feel that my poems leave a trail like the seasons. My poems flutter like leaves in autumn and return to the earth, and then may bloom in the spring of the hearts that encounter them.

We are all connected. I feel that deeply. The Beloved contains us All, and each of us is called to our own heart's way of expressing this. So I naturally have deep respect for each person's path and their heart guidance and pray for its realization in each life.

The Thrill of Creating

In the silence of morning before dawn
feeling the energy of the stream
of creating
as we continue to let beauty
have its way with us
flowing out to the world in such joyful ways
catching that elusive beauty
that flashes into view
along the edges of vision
not looking directly at it
but letting it slip by in the dream
or in the streaming silence
between waking and sleeping
or in the enchantment of music

flowing and dancing
in and out of awareness
like the face and form and color
appearing on a canvas
or on the screen in digital play
in the words that seem to arise
out of the whiteness
and purity of the page
or out of the dark skies of the mystic night
whispering to the open heart
kissing the open hand
that holds the brush or the pen
the dear ones are there
unseen and outside of time
waiting for us to be touched
by the one caressing and kissing
our eyes
coming to life in our soul.

What Used To Be

by Edith Lazenby

The practice of writing eases and opens, giving me a way to let go and look inside and see how I am feeling what I'm feeling, and maybe help me to just *let it be.*

I think this piece, called "What Used To Be" speaks for itself. Such is my day: thinking of *what used to be,* noticing the old tapes that don't play but sit there like friends I used to enjoy, in an odd way.

My writing process is a meditation on being. The Muse guides my heart and my hands move. The connection I long for meets me halfway, and what I missed knowing lands like a blossom at my feet. And then I feel a little better and know there are many who have been here with me, in their own way.

What Used To Be

Used to be I'd crawl into a hole.
Used to be, I'd wish
To die while I cried.
Used to be I'd hear
Voices echo worthlessness
Through a worm's belly,
Words would tease
Me into not caring
Because what really matters
When the insides are tied
Into knots with wires
Scraping my heart
And jabbing my stomach?
My eyes hurt from trying
To find what is not here.
Used to be, I'd roll over
With sunrise and pull the covers
Up to my ears so I could not
Hear birds chirping, kids playing.
Used to be I'd lie in bed till evening
And wish night would leave as soon
As it came. Used to be meaning
Came with a story of what is not.
Now I sit with hands wrapped
Around prayer to help me unfold
What I cannot control, ease the angst
Of what I cannot know, soothe the fear
Of realizing all that matters is right here:
This breath, clouds in the sky,
Kitty by my side, kitchen full of dishes,
Home that wants love as much as I want
To give it. What used to be haunts my window
Because when I look out I see in: the gnarled
Branches of my heart are trying to grow roots
So the life I want to live can flow.

Used to be I'd lie down and pray never to get up.
Today I sit and try to unlearn what time stole
And make that history a gift so I'll remember
Now is not how it used to be; now I am free
To create a life where I can pray and dream.
Now I shift meaning into this frame to hold
What I cannot find, touch what I do not feel,
Give what I do not have, save who I cannot lose.

Muse

by Vrinda Aguilera

A dragonfly's body, you say, riding low and heavy with iridescent flashes of purple, black and green? Ah, I see, think this if you must. As for my crisp, white shirt, with cuffs of lace and buttons of pearls? Did you catch a glimpse of that? A dandelion puff or wisp of cloud? Maybe.

Or could it be that you have just caught sight out of the corner of your eyes of the spirit of the muse?

Muse

I blow in on the sultry
End of summer breeze
Riding humid currents,
Darting between raindrops with ease

I float in on the warm,
Wet morning mist
Shedding my blankets of fog
Dawn heralding my daily trysts

It is I, your muse,
hear me sing
Melodies of the moment

A breath of air in the spring

It is I, your muse
Whispering fragments of truth
Casting spells of inspiration
Fueled on ancient elixirs of youth

What, you do not recognize me?
Well, I've always been at your side
Prodding and poking
Even when you'd rather I hide

Why do you not hear me?
Instead you'd rather ignore?
Listen, just listen,
I most humbly implore

My voice is like honey
My hands deft and smooth
I spin spider webs into silk
Towering mountains I do move

I live in the shadows
I bathe in vast seas
I sleep in humble porch flowerpots
Like a kite I drift with the breeze

Hear the music in my laughter
A graceful dance your steps will know
Pat attention to my counsel
From your pen prolific prose will flow

I turn sand into castles
Rough stones into shining jewels
I weave reeds into baskets
With nary an instrument or tool

I am your muse!

I am your whimsy!
I'm ancient, mischievous, and full of wit
I am your ruse!
I am your fancy!
Leave your window cracked open
I'll visit your dreams and stay
At least for a bit.

I Shall Be Messy

by Sarah Courtney Dean

I have always believed that poetry is painting with words. An artist friend posted somewhere saying: "When did she become a messy painter" and my muse flew!

I Shall Be Messy and Profligate With Words

I shall be messy and profligate with words today!
I shall paint you cerulean skies,
with white and grey clouds..
And love the color of blood.
I shall be messy and profligate with words today.
I shall paint you spring green trees,
with baby pink blossoms.
And love the color of blood.
I shall be messy and profligate with words today.
I shall paint you a foamy green sea
with white cavorting gulls.
And love the color of blood
Dripping from the palette of my heart.

Closing In

by Pranada Comtois

O n my fiftieth birthday I was walking on the shore of the
Atlantic Ocean and spotted a diver in the water. I immediately
remembered my days of scuba diving off the coast of Santo Domingo
when I was sixteen. The gulf of years between sixteen and fifty became
pronounced, but even more poignantly, I realized that it was time for
me to accept that I had passed through youth. It was a stark, sinking
sensation of moving from denial into an uncomfortable truth.

This is the first poem I ever wrote. I had never thought of myself as
a poet, and the thought of writing a poem never occurred to me. These
lines came out spontaneously. I felt quite awkward when my esteemed
writing friend, a poet herself, declared me "Poet Pranada," but her
confidence in me gave me permission to write other poems.

My relationship with my writing mentor has convinced me that
each of us women should go out of our way to help each other find our
voice and release it into the world.

Closing In

Diver bobbing
In grey-brown-green water
red & white flag moving
almost imperceptibly
like years wearing out a body.

Waves rush into yellow-brown crests
that peak and crash
into tan caps
that struggle against
a south-easterly wind
whipping
the flap-edge of the silver umbrella

into a wrestle sound,
softer than
branches & twigs
against a window pane
more soothing than
the physic jolt
this instant
grown into a moment,
several strung together into minutes
stopped sudden
facing stark

youth is gone forever.

Light's Cover Is A Root
by Edith Lazenby

I write from this impermanent place; it is deep yet runs through me moment by moment. I write often and don't remember what inspired this moment per se, but this piece, to me, is about the strength of the spirit: sometimes fed by darkness but living in light.

My poem is also a metaphor for the creative process, where I begin by going in, without knowing where I'll end up. It may seem like a maze but actually I find it is a direct line, via the Muse, through me, to what I find. And I have learned that what is there is also -in its own way- in others. I hope to reach you by speaking with integrity, from my heart, to yours.

Light's Cover Is A Root

I begin tugging at a root.
Its top reaches beyond
Moon, and its bottom
Goes so far under I cannot

Touch what it feeds.
Yet the trunk, the body
Holds this core strong
As a Redwood.
More than mountain,
Deep as Earth's clay.
My heart pulses
Blood of light; sparkles
And shines, and yet
Within the dark,
In light's absence,
Need fresher than a baby's
Demanding each moment
Be fed as an egg
Ready to hatch a life,
As if now a cocoon
Allowing a caterpillar to die
So a butterfly can fly,
As if it a grave
Promising light,
This root holds
What I cannot find:
A ground that knows
Love and fear cannot live
Side by side, for moment
By moment I choose
A life that feeds a spirit
Death cannot deny.

Savor the Sensations

by Mary McManus

I feel so blessed by my gift of poetry. Poetry enables me to move beyond the trauma of my past into a place of light, love, joy, peace, happiness and freedom. This is a poem of contrasts. In order to live a full, rich, vibrant life - we need to embrace and then release all experiences, especially the dark ones.

Savor The Sensations

The bitter taste of trauma seasoned by salty tears
must be savored in equal measure
as hot cocoa slowly sipped wrapped in a warm, soft sweatshirt
reminiscent of hugs surrounding by friends in the sanga
seasons and sensations come and go
when we allow nature to just be
not holding on
or avoiding
gentle embrace.

In the darkness of winter
peace and solitude can be found amidst the cold
as snowflakes gently silently fall
look closely and see the glittering diamonds that will be reflected by
    the morning sun
savor the sensations
release the grip
of fear or grasping
allowing heart and mind to breathe it all in
and let it go with a deep exhale.

Serpent
by Ruth Calder Murphy

As for all poets, poetry is for me a vessel - a way, a channel - by which I am able to reflect, consolidate, heal when needed and move forward. Of course, it can also be a way to express the simplest ideas - a way of holding everyday things up to the light and enjoying the way they sparkle.

For me, this poem holds elements of all the reasons I write. It's a reflective poem, looking at my self and how I deal with life, how as human beings we all, to an extent, manifest elements of the serpent, in the way we get knocked back and damaged and need to crawl into our holes for a while before shedding that old skin and moving on to bask in the sunlight again.

It's also a celebration of life and the fact that we are part of the circle of life, a constant dying and rising again - every new moment, reborn. In many mythologies, the serpent is a symbol of these things. The East, in Native-American Shamanism, is linked with Spirit and with the Eagle totem - with being able to rise above and see the bigger picture.

Serpent

I shed my skin, snake that I am,
serpent coiled in the setting sun.
I turn around and the world has changed
and my body crawls from its shell again.

Asleep on the rock in the heat of the day,
I bask in the light 'til the sun slides away.
I slip to the hollow under the stone
when the west claims the sun and the daylight is gone.

I look to the past, to the scales I have shed
in the light of the seasons, now lying dead
and I know as I look where the new days dawn,
with the skin that is lost my hope is reborn.

When We Hit the Wall

by Jenn Grosso

The ebb and flow of the creative process presents us with two very different ways of looking at the times of stillness: It can feel like a dreaded curse, or an invitation to enter our soft inner cocoon and transform, even just a little.

This poem is for everyone who has ever felt stuck, lost and hopeless, and is a reminder that only in the darkness can we see the stars.

When We Hit The Wall

The landscape before us changes
    There is an unbearable stillness
    In the air that grows stale and wretch
    All colors fade and retreat

The great expanse curls and shrivels
    Dries up on itself and shrinks
    Hardened and cruel
    Into the wall before us pressing tightly

The air grows thicker and thicker
    Gasping and panicking we scream
    Our bloody fingers scratching
    For freedom beyond this confinement

We look up and see the engulfing dark sky above
    Stars shining brighter than ever before
    Amazed and bewildered we stare
    And see the same stars in each other's eyes

We remember once again the greatest truth
    Of the magnificent illusion
    The continuous nature of time and space
    Our hurried heartbeats begin to slow

Suddenly the hard and jagged walls soften
    Surrounding us instead like a blanket
    Warm and gentle beckoning us to rest
    Our healing cocoon holding us safely

When we hit the wall
       It can be hard, cold and cruel
       Or softly inviting us to transformation
       Until we emerged anew into the world

The whole world is whispering:
Listen - in the trees,
in the tumbling, turning leaves,
in the spiraling seasons
and the ocean breeze.

Ruth Calder Murphy

2

Nature

Across the ages, poets have related to natural phenomena as a reflection of our own human experience. We hear our moans in the wind, see our freedom in the flight of birds, inhale our passions in flowers, and taste our tears in seawater. With senses highly attuned to our surroundings, poets thrive in natural environments, for Nature's primal beats never fail to effortlessly rouse a sensitive heart and usher it toward poetry.

Plato valued the role of poets as recorders of life's beauty: beauty that political historians usually missed. In a language that resonates with the trickling of streams and the buzzing of bees, poets translate Nature's symphonies into words, but never without adding the sounds of their own instruments into the composition. In the process, the contemplative soul lets her sentiments be swayed by the seasons and electrified by lightening. In doing so, the poet discovers a sense of divine oneness, wedding us to a wonderous reality.

Of all the muses that breathed life into these poems, perhaps it's not surprising then that the one that did so most consistently was Nature. With her rhythms and cycles, her calmness and storms, the natural world around us seems to be powerfully tethered to the emotional landscapes swirling within the hearts of these poets. So when their poems emerged, they inevitably rose like suns, and fell like rain, and splashed out in waves of metaphorical expression that drew faint lines between where nature ended and the poet began.

Nature offers us such a variety of colors and textures that it's not difficult to see ourselves in it: to recognize our own depths in her seas, and our own elevations in her mountains. Poets' hearts set out on expeditions in nature to uncover the mysteries of their own beings and map out trails to inner treasures. When surrounded by nature we spontaneously mine our spiritual core and delight in the dynamic dialogue between the divine inside of us and the divine that surrounds us. Our poems inevitably become the dance of the two.

The inner terrain of a female heart swells with qualities that mimic those in nature. It is both soft and strong, gentle yet fierce, and beating with nourishment that flows out to feed us. When the feminine heart is neglected, so is life itself. Consequently, these poems draw poignant parallels between restoring an ecological balance to our planet and honoring feminine wisdom, for they illumine the indisputable interdependence that exists between our inner and outer geographies.

In this chapter we hear women's voices draw from dawn, merge with the sun's orbit, decode messages in the songs of birds and sympathize with vanishing bees. As the poets listen to the whispering universe, trees are befriended, rainfall beckons, moonbeams heal and souls settle by the sea: all blessings as seen through their eyes. And even as they are struggling to burst from cocoons and escape blizzards, these poets experience connection with divinity, finding holiness even in long, dark winters filled with the smallest snowflakes: reflections of a sacred geometry the women themselves know they belong to. Nothing could be more exhilarating. Their poems express this.

Dawn

by Shahla Ghobadi

To me, Dawn is about windows through which we receive things in life. It is about observing that life, as an ongoing wonder, regenerates itself.

I wrote this poem because I have always loved looking at windows and thinking about life in general. I found this a very calming experience, which leads me feeling 'this moment is all there is".

Dawn

Just before the dawn,
we may sit on the bed
and look at the cold,
leaking through the window,
melting right where it falls off.

Just like the water,
with its honest composition,
through the same window,
sun will begin to find
our sensitive skin again.

When next morning spreads over the window,
Let's sit again, let's behold
all that comes in, all that is coming,
you may see,
neither the cold nor the warmth
have remained the same
by next morning.

Salute to the Sun in the Infinite Embrace

by Ruth Calder Murphy

Anyone who's ever experienced yoga will almost certainly know the Salute to the Sun. It's one of the most all-encompassing and, for me at least, energizing and at the same time calming sequences.

Every day, I try to set aside some time - at the same time early every morning - to be what I think of as "Physically Spiritual". A time when I try to engage my body, mind and spirit together in a holistic activity that brings me to a better experience of wholeness than I awoke with.

Sometimes, I run. Sometimes I work out. Almost always, I do some yoga - even just a few minutes.

Salute to the Sun is special. As I stretch high, I connect to Spirit. As I bend low, I connect to Earth. Touching my toes, I'm reminded of the *Ouroboros* - the constant circle and cycle of birth and life and death and rebirth.

This poem is one of several that links with a painting of mine, called "The Infinite Embrace", that features the Ouroboros, the Sun, the Moon, and the Tree of Life - powerful symbols in many traditions. When I Salute the Sun, I feel connected to all these things - physical and metaphorical - and a part of something wonderful.

Salute to the Sun in the Infinite Embrace

Stretching high,
I inhale
the metamorphosis
of today
and exhale every yesterday
that lingers
in cobwebbed sleep
and shadowed memory.
My fingers reach to the re-born sky,
exulting in the freedom of blossoming branches,
unfurling leaves
and deep,
mud-mothered roots,
where womb-red fire
pulses and warms.
Bending double,
mouth to tail,
I am the constant circle.
Another inhale,
I am

the infinite sky,
the profound
Eternal sigh.
Here I am,
ever I,
in the Infinite Embrace.

Message of the Birds

by Carolyn Riker

My garden is small and has very little definition. I let plants reseed. There's little strategy involved and that is good. I enter a different sense of time when in nature. On this day, I was trimming a massive, heirloom, climbing rose. There were sparrows and a pair of goldfinches entertaining me. As I settle into the garden's rhythm, it becomes meditative. The birds were speaking and I listened.

Message of the Birds

As she stepped lightly through the sodden moss,
The wind whispered.
It was a space between the shadows and light.
She blinked to see if she really saw, and there it was:
> A reflection of her soul in the veins of a leaf,
> An ancient image of color and form,
Breathing, like a fern, through her pores.
She floated to the treetops with the birds.
Liltingly, she danced in the wind.
Wordlessness transferred to her eye, mind and soul,
The Sparrow said,
> "Listen."
The Finch tilted her head and said,
> "What is here isn't. This is a spiritual quest.

It's a matter of seeing between the dot and the blur, the love
and the fear
It's a space....between a leaf, a flutter and a breeze."
And she knew...as soft and real as the moss where she stood,
Truth had been translated in their song.
Life was in motion,
Awakened and renewed.

Springtime Meditation
by Shailie Dubois

The earthly seasons mirror the seasons of our spiritual journey. Each season is essential to fully experience the deep healing, wonder, and awe of God. Winter pulls us inwards and offers an opportunity to see the shadows that keep the God-given seeds from blossoming in our hearts. Spring is creating fertile soil for the new seeds to sprout. Summer gifts us with the light to rapidly grow towards the sun. Fall is a time of celebration to welcome the community and share the abundance within your sacred garden.

This poem is inspired by the transition from winter to spring. Surrendering to the seasonal ebbs and flows, contractions and releases, God's love and light flow into our hearts, nourishing us and inspiring our true selves to flourish.

Springtime Meditation

Loving Creator,
Thaw the winter chills,
Melt away the shadows,
Wash the settled dust.

With this soil,
Plant a garden in my heart,
Awaken your gifted seeds,
Blossom my truest self.

With this being,
Shine,
Speak,
Dance,
Play,
Love...through me.

Nature's Symphony

by Sarah Courtney Dean

Part of being a Druid for me is that all things are connected: Each rock, tree, bird, animal, and human being joined in this dance we call life. Not one being more important than the other, each with a part to play in the greater scheme, which is to honor our Mother.

Nature's Symphony

Rushes heavy with their
Summer heads
Bend with the breeze
Alive
With warbling birds
Not
Exactly
Singing
As this could be called a song
But it is praise
To the
Creator.
And I find peace
Where nature meets
The creator's brush
Alive
In all creation
Living

Breathing
Life
Begetting more life in a colorful symphony
Alive with her sounds
Alive with
Her

The Tree

by Jyoti Rebecca

I have felt like a nomad, a gypsy all my life – always searching, never finding. An outsider wherever I went. It manifested as a constant movement, first from one country to another during my teenage years, and then as a constant searching for something out there, in the world, that would complete me, that would end this existential angst.

The poem "The Tree" is a metaphor for the One who has manifested the multiplicity of forms and has remained centered and grounded within Its Absolute Knowingness and Beingness. The trunk of a tree is solidly rooted in the ground and yet its branches are looking heavenly into the sky. This is the longing, the yearning to know the Self while living in this body.

The Tree

I sit unwavering
The trunk of a tree
Nothing touches me
I am unbound
Centered and free

I am the tree
The giver of life
That grows to give solace
Water and food

To every soul
That wanders by

I am the tree
That grows big and strong
So that you know I am
That I Am
The Tree of Life

A Maple Tree in My Heart
by Shahla Ghobadi

This poem relates to my experience on the importance of perseverance in tough times. It is about how seasons change and how better times will come, naturally. It is about what makes a difference.

In this poem, I talk to my 8-year-old niece. I tell her how we will have more meaningful dialogue when she grows older. I tell her about the stillness of a single grass and how we can learn from her.

A Maple Tree in My Heart

Another spring is breaking out
And I feel a maple tree growing inside my heart
It is celebrating the season, making sweet golden sap inside
I bless the winter nights that nourished my heart
Some time when you grow older, when you become a woman
Sit with me; ask me what made a difference
In keeping the light in heart and vision
In feeling gratitude, in plain dark days and nights
I will listen to you, and you will listen to us
We can then turn down and look at a silent grass
Knowing how it keeps its stillness over years, million years
You will then know we have a similar story
Together, we should plant a seed of peace

Doesn't matter which season it is
We will feel the unfolding universe of light- again and again.

The Song of the Trees
by Vrinda Aguilera

It's a beautiful fall day and the weather is crisp and bright. The sun is shining golden, warming the edges of everything. I have a day off and decide to take myself out on a date to lunch and then to the park to write.

Upon arriving at the park I head up an unfamiliar path and find, much to my delight, a newly created nature area. A rock garden anchors one side with tall, multi leveled, cut cylinder stones arranged artfully, haphazardly, imbuing the area with the simplicity and serenity of a Zen garden. At another end is a brick outlined, red pebble bed labyrinth-perfect for the contemplative walker. I make a note to meander the spirals of its maze in my bare feet. The symmetry and *mandala* like geometry of the circular clearing appeals to me, and sets about to define the space as one which invites contemplating, meditating or quiet strolling. 'Come here, sit here, walk here,' it seems to say.

Newly planted, young trees are planted at judiciously spaced intervals. They rest in carefully created beds, tucked up with blankets of pine needles, tended by the hands of some nurturing gardener souls, sharing their care and service with the sentient beings that plant life is. The place is new but this is ok, as we were all once new many times over. There is a certain mystery and potential that newness invites. It holds a space pregnant with possibilities, it's toes edging against the invisible starting line of the unknown future.

All of this is encircled by mature woods. Lacy edged shadows decorate the tree line where the sun filters through the perimeter. There, standing watch at the edge of the forest are the tree elders, draped with their robes of Spanish moss, majestically sheltering and watching the newness with their ancient, upraised arm branches. Silent witnesses to all that is around them.

How do they converse with one another, these trees, winks from their knotted trunks? Dry cracks and rustlings when the wind rushes through their foliage? Well, how about their roots- perhaps their root systems from which they derive nourishment from Florida's rich, albeit sandy, soil also serves as a channel for communications with one another. I can imagine vibrations through the loamy earth, being sent forth at subtle, varying rates to be a language of sorts. Or do they simply embrace the limitations and solitude inherent in their plant bodies- as veritable living lessons in patience, tolerance, forbearance, acceptance and humility?

When was the last time you saw a tree abusing another or refusing to bend with the natural force of a strong wind? Who is the person who has witnessed a tree withholding his God given gifts of shelter and shade to one who asked it of him, regardless of their life form- be it the small ant or proud man? That's right, never! Trees do not discriminate. Oh, grandfathers, grandmothers, mothers and fathers- I see you! I honor and respect your service and bearing.

The longer I sit here the more I seem to become aware of the texture and depth of the natural atmosphere. There is an ethereal exchange occurring if I am quiet enough, still enough, I can hear it. The young trees seem to speak in a different language- their leaves haven't yet dried, their tender trunks are supple and bendy and thus their voices are different: quieter, softer. As an approaching wind blows I hear it being heralded with the other voices of trees farther out in the forest, not unlike that of an incoming ocean wave sweeping through the foliage, crowns of trees bustle and rustle with news and announcements. Some are singing, mocking the twitter of feathered birds, flitting about somewhere out of sight. A poem flows effortlessly as I hear the voices of the trees and the message they deliver to me.

The Song of the Trees

I hear the song of the trees
I hear the sound of the trees
Offering counsel to me
Whispering advice
Sharing their lessons of patience,
Humility and tolerance

'Have courage
Seek faith
Align yourself with grace
Your roots in the earth
Stay grounded
With your arms raised towards the skies
Embrace heaven's gifts and eternity

Those that bend the most do not break
Yielding is not a sign of weakness
It's an art of faith'

I hear the songs of the trees
They whisper their secrets to me

'When great torrential rainstorms
Open up above and the force of a thousand
Gale windstorms blow from all sides
Rejoice!
Dance in the downpour
Seize the moment and let go
Move to the melody of the pitter, patter
Pulsate to the staccato of the thunder
Our leaves release their most beautiful
Scents when caught in the storm

When you are drenched, drink it in!
Be satiated and quench your thirst

When the sun sets, sleep
Dawn rising sees us stretching our branch arms
Scratching our itches and greeting the day
We bathe in the morning dew and are serenaded by visiting birds

We take our refreshments effortlessly
From the glowing Sun
The moisture all around
The nourishing brown soil of the earth

Life is simple
Celebrate with us!'

Rain

by Braja Sorensen

This village of Mayapur that is my home is a town of temples, of sacred songs, poetic chants, rhythmic melodies, and whispered prayers. Its beauty lies in the earth, in the colors of its fields, the greenness of its trees, the ever-changing drama of its skies, the depths of its rivers, the lilting songs of the many birds that sing from morning 'til nightfall...and most especially in the hearts of its people.

At every moment there is something waiting to be seen not with the eyes alone, but with the heart, the soul: the sound of a bird, bursts of rain, a beautiful sunrise, a jackal's howl in the night. As I watch the days unfold from my window that looks over the fields, every seemingly ordinary event becomes extraordinary, every person special, every moment a blessing. The caterpillar thinks of becoming a butterfly and so is transformed into a butterfly in the same life. In the same way, as I drink in the deliciousness of my surroundings, I want to be transformed by the beauty of this place, want that it's glorious qualities enter my heart.

This morning I watched a person in a colorful streak of red in the distance, making way across the fields, upper body covered by an umbrella, moving carefully through acres and acres of green grass, rice paddies, and tiny little walkways made slippery by the rain. After a while, I could see that it was a woman, and as she deftly navigated the rainy fields, I saw she held a baby in her left arm. I watched the beauty and grace with which she moved, heard her voice quietly singing, too quietly and too distant to hear what she sang....and I thought of the Sanskrit verses from ancient Vedic scriptures that describe so poetically how, in the spiritual world, every word is a song, every step a dance, and every rain storm a blessing:

Rain

You called my name
I came
No question
But gave myself
Freely
Harder and harder
Drenching

Wondrous fat buckets of moisture
Ploughing into the earth
You wanted this
You asked for it
Begged for it
Here I am

You love the sound of
My voice
Music to your ears you said
Luscious, loud and satisfying
Hear me, then,
I'm singing for you
You asked
I sang...

I can sing all night

I will
You love it
Some don't
They berate the sound of me
Lament my presence
Curse the after effects
The echo of my song
For them I am like tears
No joy...

Rain
Rain
Rain

Whispering

by Ruth Calder Murphy

The whole world is whispering - whispering long-lost truths and the mysteries of connection. At least, this is what I'm coming to believe. Myths and legends repeat the same themes and these are echoes of what we see in nature and the circle of life... And the really exciting thing, it seems to me, is that I'm a part of it: we are a part of it.

I'm part of the whispering and singing and dancing and being and sometimes, I can almost touch it, before it spins off again. Wherever I am, I'm where the whispers meet, because they meet in me - and in you, and in every living thing.

Whispering

The whole world is whispering:
Listen - in the trees,
in the tumbling, turning leaves,
in the spiraling seasons
and the ocean breeze.
The whole world is whispering,

susurrating, rustling,
Listen - it's the whisper of the Winter freeze,
the dancing of the Spring time,
the languor of the Summer,
the rolling of the Autumn
and the tumbling, turning leaves...
The whole world is whispering
and I will be listening;
listening and whispering
and susurrating, murmuring -
filling my being with the whispering of everything,
the song of becoming and being and living -
and the whispering's
becoming the song of belonging...
The whole world's singing
the song of transformation,
the song of evolution,
the song of re-creation
and the song of resurrection...
Listen, listen, listen -
there is music in the rhythm,
there is rhythm in the dancing -
and the whole world is dancing
- the whole world is dancing
to the rhythm and the beat -
and the whole world is singing
to the spinning of the spheres
and I am dancing,
dancing,
where the whispers meet.

For the Bees

by Camellia Stadts

I believe that there is a deep connection between bees and the Blessed Mother (Mary, Tara, or any other form you chose to see her as).

I wrote this a few months back while doing a research paper on bees and colony collapse disorder for an English class I was taking. I realized that everything that is going on with the bees and the whole planet Earth, can be summed up in just 5 words: *Total lack of the sacred.* One night this poem just came pouring out of me.

I live just on the outskirts of Detroit, Mi and have no land for a garden much less room to tend bees as much as I would like to. But I will continue to study and write about bees.

For the Bees

Look under petals
Around the block
Down concrete highways
Through Mall parking lots

Where have we gone?
Left without a trace
We could no longer keep up
Your demanding pace

You take us to places
We don't even know
And expect us to call
Wherever you dump us, home.

The pesticides used
You could not understand
Goucho, Poncho
They need to be banned

The sugar water you feed us
Will not keep us strong
More poison you give us
All winter long

So where have we gone?
You ask scratching your heads
We are in the Divine Mothers arms
Where we are safe from all harm.

You will not think to look there
You are no longer wise
Your arrogance has blinded you
To your own demise.

Moonbeam Repair

by Anita Brown

Enjoying the view from my backyard hot tub, I gazed at the moon. It was hanging in the sky as if for the first time. I began to sense this poem forming in me as an act of healing a deep, old wound.

This was the beginning for me of finding that all of nature wants to communicate with us...we just need to stay aware and enjoy and absorb the gentle whisper in our spirits.

Moonbeam Repair

broke my own barely-beating heart
went un- noticed
let alone fatal

pain endured then absorbed, changing its shape
until it appeared- a floating disconnect

once full and impervious
two halves forming the whole
self-righteous and solid
closed to the light

suddenly cracked and imperfect, at the ready
for the outpouring of emotion
tumbling through tumult

at the ready for the laser-bright white beam
through half-slit eyes
travels through eternity
to pierce my chest
and fills the cracks like mortar
a healing, translucent balm
and now by osmosis
gives and receives
the blood-red agape love
worthy of the creator
of the moon and stars
and earth and sky

The Moon is Still Silver

by Victoria Erickson

This poem partly stems from my fierce connection with nature, and from the sky, and partly from my fascination with how we hold things in our bodies long after they're gone.

I've also always been amazed by the simple concept that the earth will continue to spin no matter what type of heartbreak is happening or how much we long for it to stop. That's the thing about life, really. We need to keep going, and we need to find some relief from the beauty around us.

The Moon is Still Silver

"I meant to tell you
the moon is still silver.
It still rises same as it used to rise,

42

shedding light onto cities and lands
softened by the coming of night.

I meant to tell you that I still gaze up,
same as when you were here,
and that in the stillest of hours
while carrying a heart
as wide as the sea,
if I soak in that moon,
it may bring some relief.

I meant to tell you that
I still taste your song in me.
It comes in waves
under silent skies,
It threatens my sanity.

How you came and you went
long before I could tell you
I didn't want you
to leave.

But you did.
And the moon is still silver.

So here I stand
left with echoes
of us
And those nights
that used
to breathe."

My Soul Settles by the Sea

by Mary McManus

Last summer I spent a lot of time at Carson Beach in South Boston. I remember the first day it was low tide and I went to walk out to the water. There was what looked like pimples on the mud. Upon closer examination, I realized that they were baby snails - thousands and thousands of them. I didn't want to risk stepping on any one so I gingerly returned to my beach chair patiently -or initially not so patiently- waiting for the tide to come back in.

As I sat, my first thought was that I was hot and wanted to go into the water. My feet were all muddy - yuck! Could the tide please hurry up and come back in? And I smiled and laughed warmly with myself. I felt so blessed that I could open my heart and Spirit to receive the gift of that moment. I chose to use that time for a meditation.

At first blush, the snails looked like nothing more than pimples of mud. How quick we can be to dismiss and miss out on so much in the world because we allow appearances to deceive us. These beautiful vulnerable creatures were there as a sign from the Divine.

As a polio survivor in a long leg brace in first grade, I was dismissed and demeaned always chosen last believing that I was less than because of what happened to my body. No one saw the beauty that was still me. No one cherished or honored my being just as I was. As I look back on it - wouldn't it have been magnificent if another child could have walked slowly by my side and together we could have taken the time to cherish the simple joys of nature. So much value is placed on running around, accomplishing, doing and we miss out on so much of life. We miss out on the time to just, sit and be in the moment.

Mother Nature taught me a wonderful lesson that day. It is so important to cherish and embrace all sentient beings. Each flower, each animal and each person has so much to teach us when we open our hearts to the wonder of it all. Nature moves in her own pace and rhythm one that is untouched by the 'will' and desire of a human. Life becomes incredibly more peaceful, and wonder-filled once we surrender to what is; taking peace and comfort in knowing that all is exactly as it should be.

My Soul Settles by the Sea

Pimples
shell-less snails
finding their way through the muck and mire
one speed – slow – for these Divine creatures
vulnerable at low tide
living in the moment
no expectations
no wishing the tide would hurry up
bemoaning their fate.

Steadfast and sure
known mudfilled mission
wordless fearless world
knowing only how to be
basking in the sun.

Gentle breeze
my heart beats
synchs with nature's soundtrack
breathing fully
deeply
at a snail's pace
peace

my soul settles by the sea.

Inner Selkie

by Freya Watson

There is a folktale common to many traditions about a fisherman who falls in love with a seal woman (called Selkie in some countries). While she has shed her skin and is sitting unaware, he grabs and hides it leaving her no option but to follow him home. Over time, she bears him several children. One day, her youngest child finds the hidden skin while the father is away from home and shows it to his mother. Seeing the skin again reawakens her to her true self and she returns to the sea.

This poem is one I wrote on a blustery autumn night when I was out under the stars feeling a pull to the wild, away from the responsibilities of children, home and career. It was like a sweet longing that tugged on my gut and wouldn't leave me alone. I honored it with this poem that night and then booked myself some time off the next day!

Being in touch with that untamed part of me is an essential part of my life that always brings me back to my soul – and making time to heed the call of the wild is part of a deep commitment I have made to my spirituality.

Inner Selkie

That wildness calls me again,
Drawing me home;
My seal skin left too long
Is demanding to be worn.
But how does it smell,
This call of the wild?
Like the salty, restless sea
On a stormy night.
And how does it sound,
This call of the wild?

Like branches tossing in a storm
Wanting to take flight.
But how does it feel,
This call of the wild?
Like warm wind on bare skin
One dark autumn night.

Watercourse

by Pranada Comtois

For the first twenty years of my mantra meditation practice I envisioned reaching a specific goal. I kept thinking it would be right around the corner, until one day I let go and gave up thinking about "results." This is how I envisioned my journey afterward.

Watercourse

It's entirely possible for the daily hours
  with beads in hand
  chanting *Shri Nam*

to glide along
  the wet slide
  of pleasure and ease

not unlike a youthful river
  of showers and snowmelt
  surging over stones

coursing to its destination
  the point invisible
  from here

the waterway

wends
  meandering bends

is in no conscious hurry
  to pass through
  lower or higher elevations

it's going

it's going.

Unstuck

by Nancy Alder

After weeks of being unable to move forward and feeling trapped by my small community and aspects of my life I got stuck at home in Blizzard Nemo. I was not figuratively stuck, like I was in my professional life, but rather literally stuck at my house. We were buried in three feet of snow and unable to leave for 48 hours until our plow guy came.

Surprisingly the freedom that came from being unable to leave gave me great wisdom about what was keeping me paralyzed in my career. The softness and freedom of the snow was inspirational, and the confinement with my family a gift.

This poem was a result of the weekend, the snow and its wisdom. I feel less stuck. I feel lighter and focused. I appreciate what I am and what I have to give. I am finding my wings.

Unstuck

the floating snowflakes
dropped weightless to the ground.

the roof, the grass and the roads

were soon buried under their mass.

steps were tough, driving impossible
leaving was not an option.

I was stuck.

the glue came not via the snow,
it was from fear to move forward.

fear of the unknown is heavier
than three feet of wet snow.

fear of failure is more paralyzing
than the unplowed driveway.

heaviness, stickiness, stuck.

snowflakes celebrate their uniqueness and
glide effortlessly in their own ways.

it is as if snowflakes are made
of feathers and a blizzard is their wings.

the road reappeared and the snow is melting,
and because of the snow I feel less stuck.

i have learned from the snowflakes
to release the hesitations and fear.

I am finding the lightness in my own feathers

I am appreciating my uniqueness and offerings.

I am trusting that I will soar and land softly.

I am finding my wings.

I am unstuck.

Surrender

by Mary Mc Manus

Last Spring I was sitting in my yard in meditation. I watched a monarch butterfly dancing on the lawn and felt an amazing connection to this beautiful creature. She invited me to contemplate my journey of transformation as I had set out on an adventure to heal my life.

Just as the caterpillar has to die to be transformed, I experienced a death of my old ways, my old habits, of fear and of living in the shadow of myself afraid to express and experience the fullness of my Being. I was touched by grace and found amazing healers and teachers flow into my life once I set my intention to heal.

When I run, I express the fullness of my transformation living in the present moment leaving behind all that went before dancing with the butterfly the Divine dance of mystery and sacredness.

Surrender

No longer living life in retreat
hiding in the bunker
cowering, quivering, shivering
mustering courage
waving the white flag
a magnet for the light.

Pain pulsating
wringing out fear from every cell
space for love
exchange of love
end to torment of sleepless nights
tortured twisted thoughts
move forward....

plodding along on diminutive legs unnoticed

steadily stealthily moving forward in its journey
undeterred
undistracted
fulfilling its destiny in the Divine Plan
the caterpillar surrenders.

Weaving its temporary tomb entering the darkness
trusting
time suspended in the tomb womb
no choice but to be
just be as the mystery unfolds.

Relinquishing old ways
appendages absorb absolve
disquieting discomfort
unsettling uncertainty
seemingly never ending suspense

U N T I L

the beauty moment of freedom arrives

lighting on the lawn
wings flapping
she invites me to celebrate
warming sun
buds on trees
winter darkness a distant memory.

Orange and black bespeckled
bejeweled with Divine Love
glistening in all her glory---

Come dance with me
As I run I move with the majesty of the monarch
I rise to salute the sun
open grateful heart
rejoicing
relishing freedom.

Offering on an Autumn Day

by Nancy Carlson

I was inspired to write this poem on the Fall Equinox. It was a beautiful quiet day for me, of going back in. It is that time of year, and it is that Time.

In the fall I am overcome by this feeling of an offering, of sorts, of my whole being: body, mind, soul, senses and emotions. It happens inwardly, yet is also reflected outwardly: an expression of all those parts of me.

Autumn is this quiet time within where I wait –the whole of me— for this Love to come. What better reason, then, to write this poem, as it comes through me!

Offering on an Autumn Day

Red and orange leaves
blowing in the wind.
Grey skies,
the bluish color of my eyes.
Fall arrives
the season of my birth,
at home in the cool Autumn air.
Wrapped in fine cloth,
hues of red, orange
blue and brown.
Soft pale skin
and golden hair.

It is the time
to go back in.
Larimar-like blue eyes
that see so much
beyond the seen.
Like a tiger

in the grass, waiting...

Grounded in this time
of season changed.
Comfortable with a cup of tea,
book in hand
and smell of wind.

A drop of Mercy...
my heart, filled
with more Love
than I can imagine.
As I walk quietly,
like the tiger,
soft, firm steps
strong body, golden fur,
watching, listening.

Grace abounds...
How could one not
know this Love
is always there?
And my heart
does not know
how much more
it could hold.
Yet, my Beloved comes,
I know nothing more...

Rest on Leaves

by Maureen Kwiat Meshenberg

Autumn is my favorite season. It calls to me as the shift of this
season transforms, I feel a transformation calling to me. I come to
a returning to my soul, looking deep within.

As I feel all that this season sheds; I feel a shedding too. And I feel all that I falls away, a releasing, the changes of the season of me.

Rest on Leaves

rest on leaves
that cover earth,
blending,
colors that
fold,
touching autumn's breath.
it comes with a turning,
my life not exerting-
a stillness upon me,
to settle within.
listen to the season's
hum upon the wind,
ushering a chill,
a silence to its closing,
trees now release
their garments,
now flowing
colors,
stand tall and naked-
against the dark sky.
like me,
I shed
to release,
to pause and see-
the resting of me.
it brings me to listening,
to changes beginning,
in the shifts now-
splitting,
ending
coming,

to myself seeing,
the season of me.

Harvest

by Ruth Calder Murphy

I've suffered, for many years, with a sunlight deficiency condition. It leaves me fatigued and prone to depression – especially during the winter months.

This poem visits some of my feelings at the turning of the year from summer to autumn and winter, my resolve to embrace the seasons and to impute sunshine and warmth to my life, even during the heart of the dark.

Harvest

As the days shrink
and the nights invade the space where
they should be,
I will reach
back to the heart of Summer
and bring,
cradled in my heart,
a single Solstice Sunbeam.
I will grow it,
nurture it,
feed it with candles
and fragrant oils from tropical flowers,
Yoga-stretch it
and clothe it in color
until,
in the depths
of Winter's ink-black gaze,
I reach my arms wide,

laugh aloud
and with the power
of equatorial days,
blaze;
my spirit bright,
defy the night
and with Spring in my heart
and Summer in my belly,
remove the season's bushel
and shine my light.
It has grown fat
and blooms happy
and will bear me
all the way to Beltane -
to dandelions
and daisy chains.
Before the days shrink
too far into night,
I will harvest
the light.

My Winter's Prayer

by Nancy Carlson

I am an aspiring *bhaktin* (practicing student) on the path of Bhakti Yoga. Bhakti Yoga is the yoga of devotion. This poem came as a metaphor of my inward journey in this wintertime of hibernation and contemplation. It reflects spiritual growth, trust and surrendering to this process of new life. Remembering the importance of patience, protection, time for space and growth, and to be open to Grace.

My Winter's Prayer

There lies a seed within,

deep inside one's heart,
resting in the womb of the Divine Mother.
This wintertime of hibernation is a holding place
always there, protecting, waiting
for the Springtime of life.

When the seed begins to open
to the Sun within,
we remember His Light and Love.

Nourishing, caring
for this tiny seed,
this sweet delightful bud,
the flowering of our True Self appears.

Beginning in the dark womb,
with patience and loving care,
we prepare for the Spring to come.

Vermont Snowfall
by Sheri Lindner

I do not believe I have ever experienced a holier cathedral than the woods while it is snowing. I find snow to be both romantic and religious, gorgeous and glorious. I feel like a child on a snow day from school and a traveler on a sacred pilgrimage all at once. When it is snowing, I can't remain indoors; I am drawn to be in it.

Vermont Snowfall

From a leaden desolate sky drift
these weightless stars spun of
air and water
that disappear on touch

so light
I might have dreamt them up
these gossamer prisms
holy geometries.

Though I cannot hold them
they press one against the other
lovers each to all until
they tuck right into the sides of earth,
like a starched clean sheet
on a birthing bed.

My Soul is a Winter Garden
by Carolyn Riker

In my winter garden, I see the plants resting as I breathe the mistiness of the frosty dew. I feel the wet moss underfoot. I feel the icy groundwater seep into my aching soul as I tap into a dormant leaf of my crimson heart; we share the same veins. I see myself as a garden transforming through the seasons.

My garden has stories, like we all do. I remember who gave me what plant or which ones were rescued from the half-price bin. I take home the neglected plants and tend to them like they are an extension of me. The bedraggled, brownish and limped leaf ones are often the strongest and most radiant given some love. A lot like people. Give them time and they will bloom.

I can get rather melancholy at this time of year. I become reflective and introspective too. I am looking through the gray and the bleak to find a pocket of love and light. There's uneasiness in this personal transformation. I don't particular enjoy feeling this way. I'm in limbo. I am swirling in a layered stream of decay and dust, much like my compost pile. I'm fermenting to create that rich, sweet humus: a spiritual layer to cultivate my roots.

My garden is tired and so am I. I need this long winter to refuel. As the seasons change, pruning and tending will be added to my meditation. I'm giving myself permission to rest while I listen to my heart for the sounds of spring. It's the sound of love, a *big* love filled with continuous rebirths as I meditate through this wintery refuge.

My Soul is a Winter Garden

Four corners
Four points
Like a tree
Roots solid
Branches lifted
Like the universe and infinity
The leaves swirl to an imaginary dance
The veins of life or leaf, pulsate
Even in a withered petal
Dormant in rest
Yet Alive
Hidden in slumber
Yet revealed
Our challenges are doors to be opened
Awakened leads to awareness
Change is here.

Winter Solstice

by Maureen Kwiat Meshenberg

Winter has always called to me to cocoon, to retreat inward deep into the layers of me. During winter I sit in its cold still waiting and bring myself to inner reflecting; waiting, like the cold winter earth to rebirth into newness. As we gather on the darkest of nights, let us remember that it is our light that pierces the dark with illuminating love.

Winter Solstice

winter's breath,
calls in the darkest of nights-
beauty black,
shortness of light.
the sun kisses the stars,
the moon embraces dark-
join now circle of women
our light we now spark.
circle of shes,
we who gather in singing,
bring forth the night-
in our humble existing.
we sing of the barren branch,
the cold winter wind rising-
the darkest of nights,
our intentions now binding.
fire that burns our souls to blend,
the darkest of nights-
will soon slumber and end.
each day will bring us,
to the beauty of light-
ending the longest winter night.
in its dark beauty,
we usher in the light.

I gaze into the waters of life
in the morning after
the darkest night
and there
the flame ignites.

Kiernan Antares

3

Light

There was a time, before the buzz of electricity, when human beings all around the world honored our dependent relationship to light. A time when we danced before fires, navigated by stars, and built entire civilizations around the orbits of the sun and moon. As a species, we are drawn to light much like a young sapling is: intuitively chasing light for our own growth and strength. For light awakens us, warms us, nourishes and energizes us. Light broadens our fields of awareness and often charts the course into our very self.

Clear perspectives arrive as a result of being *in* the light. So early peoples fused light with a sense of comfort and knowing. Light became a guide, an authority, a teacher and even a powerful reflection of one's own being. The more we imbibe the light flowing through the entire Universe, the more we are in harmony with the divine. Like a prism, those who possessed the qualities of light were seen as evolved souls, spiritual seers, or enlightened ones, illuminating the path for others, as they reflected their own light.

Across traditions—whether illustrated with auras or halos— human beings who had reached their full potential were depicted as having rays of light emanating from their heads or hearts. From Rumi to Gibran, poets before us have ignited dazzling images of us as being made of the very same light we seek. Such meditations ignite a sense of peace in the sensitive heart. At the speed of light, introspection suddenly feels like communication with cosmic intelligence: a sense that one's inner journey runs parallel with the trails of light cast in the world around us. To feel in synch with cosmic choreography is both soothing and enlivening to the poetic heart. For like the Universe we live in, light brings us to life.

Like birds that burst into song at dawn, and flower petals that unfold before sunlight, poetic hearts are naturally aroused by light.

Celebrating the relationship between the light flowing from celestial luminaries, and the light within us, we intuitively join the metaphysical dance humans have participated in across the ages. Perhaps, as Anais Nin once wrote, we notice the effect of light on the outside, because of how brightly our own inner lights shine. For, not unlike the tribes and civilizations that came before us, a poet enters into meaningful exchanges with archetypes of light as she seeks to illuminate her own nature, ultimately experiencing herself as one in substance with the very light to which she is drawn. Light, then, becomes an attractive mirror that reveals the self.

The voices of these women poets shine most brightly in this chapter as they speak of loving life, delighting in the present moment and experiencing an energizing oneness. These women joyfully share sensations of flowing freely from their own essence, answering the call of their souls, living in total trust and opening like a flower. With flashes of ripe realizations and metaphorical rays that beam from full hearts, their poems deliver messages of freedom, and love, and being at harmony with all existence. From describing themselves as dancing with the Universe to being played as instruments in divine hands, the inner flames of these poets burn brightly, with a glowing promise to kindle our own light as well.

A New Day
by Ruth Calder Murphy

I am and always have been an early riser. There's something about waking up early, when the day is truly new and knowing that swaths of as yet untouched time is spread out before me. I realize that I might be an enigma to many who enjoy a lie-in, and the bliss of lying under a duvet, knowing that they don't have to get up – and I can understand that too – but for me, it's getting up that I enjoy. Always before anyone else, with enough time to luxuriate in the solitude, create things and re-energize, all in the knowledge that the rest of the day is yet to come.

The sense of opportunity – of possibility – is one of my favorite things, followed by the sense of achievement at having done these things already, before the day reaches double figures...

This poem, though, doesn't only apply to me. Every day is a new day for each of us, whenever we step into it – and this is my hope, for every day: to seize it, fill it with wonder and beauty and make it a new yesterday, full of memories, with no regrets.

A New Day

This is a new day.
Its smooth perfection stretches
towards its end.
I will make footprints
and pathways,
stories
and memories
to color its emptiness.
I will seize this day
and make it explode into
colorful stars
that will burn bright
and light my way
to tomorrow.
This is a new day.
I will make it a new yesterday
where my remembered Self
can rest
without regret.

Oh World I Love You

by Rosemerry Wahtola Trommer

For many years I resisted the way things fall apart. I made a life out of holding things together. I believed that poetry could work as a kind of glue, could help me to fix problems, could help me to know.

But then, about two years ago, the world helped things fall apart so completely that I was able, at least for a moment, to see through my longing to make things neat. I could see through my desire to control the world.

Since then, poems have become more a way of unknowing. I come to the page with curiosity instead of answers. Rilke writes in "Autumn," about how this experience of surrender can lead us into "seeing" god: "And yet there is Someone, whose hands, infinitely calm, holding up all this falling." This poem is about my ongoing practice of allowing the world to be as it is without trying to reshape or recreate it.

Oh World I Love You

Oh world, I love you,
you with your roots
that thrust up through pavement,
you with your mudflows
and rock falls and storms.
See how daily you feed
and destroy me. How
gorgeous your fruits,
how merciless your gravity.
I love you, world, how
you make me and fuel me
and undo me again and again. Always
another death to die
and always a new bloom.
Never the same, always

the same. World, it feels
too proud to say I am you,
you with your splendor,
you with your grace.
I am dust and ashes.
You move me, adventure me.
World, thy will be done.
My problems are not problems.
My laws all are nonsense.
My rules, my dreams are cages.
Sometimes I forget to let you
raze me. I try to wrestle
the club from your hands.
And when the destruction
is done, I try to rebuild the walls,
not seeing you were offering me
infinity. Sometimes you first bring me milk,
then tear me down tenderly,
your hands the hands of a lover
undressing me slowly, but not
stopping with the scarf, the skirt—
taking also every idea I have,
every certainty, every word,
everything I would say is mine.
World I am rambling through
the silence you hold for me.
I am like a woman dying of thirst
who splashes the water with eager hands
instead of cupping it, raising it to her parched lips.
Oh world, I am losing my mind
and laughing about it. All language
is dust, and look, you blow it away.
Still I am talking to you, crazy,
I love you, I love you. Come wind,
catch these words, rend them
from the one who thinks
she is speaking. Let them fall
all around her like leaves.

At Oneness

by Salyna Gracie

As we travel the path set out before us, we often look to the road others have walked to guide us. Yet reading the signposts of others can only take us so far. As we search for our own true journey to spirit these resting places can become detours along the way. It is only when we turn toward our own hearts that we realize that everything we are searching for is already within us: As it always has been and always shall be.

At Oneness

Under crescent moons,
illuminated chambers of prayer,
endlessly I seek,
my Beloved.
Traveling infinite landscapes,
tireless,
guided by inner maps
through gardens of love.
Heart and feet beating the same rhythm,
whirling like dervishes,
devotion in motion,
one palm to earth one palm to heaven.
All eyes for you,
my love.
Your name a sacred mantra
echoing over ancient sands
or holy cities,
translating truths of universal longing.
As breath meets bone and blood,
spirit and soul,
radiance from within,
as you are here with me,
always.

Love

by Aparna Khanolkar

I wrote this on a rainy night in Santa Barbara, as I reflected on how The Universe is in us. I meditated on how the elements are in us, as they are in the Nature all around us. And I thought about all the ancient wisdom from all over the world that tells us that the glue that holds it all together is love. My desire is to live in the freedom of that love. I wish the same for you.

Love

Like a river that flows through Mother Earth, rain flows through me.
The Wind fans the flames of my fire. Sometimes fiercely, sometimes
    gently.
The space in me is pure potential.
Earth is sacred and deep, like the core in me.
All this is love - a magnificent inheritance
in this finite life, on this infinite Universe.
Love dwells, love flows, love surrounds, penetrates.
Cosmic, universal, heart-full, soulful.
Love expanding, contracting, birthing and dying each day.
Inhale love, exhale love.
Finite body, eternal soul.
Love seeks you, me, in every moment.
Surrender to its sweet beckoning. Soft caresses, gentle urging.
The inner temple bells are tolling.
The sacred sounds inviting.
Surrender. Be free today. Allow.
As you always have.
At your last breath, a new dawn will arise.
A sweet divine remembrance.
Sweet love.

Be The Moment

by Yasmeen Olya

Behind all the work I do there is a simple message: It is a message of 'wonder'. It is my intention to simply share my own wonder with the world. I believe that human beings' need for wonder is immense, and that through the experience of wonder we become grateful for our environment, we become in harmony with our existence and we open up.

Ultimately for me everything is in a state of "being created" therefore we are a part of that creation, the atoms and molecules have not stopped their cosmic dance and we are a part of it. We are a part of that dance, cradled in the universal tide, we are as balanced as our realization allows.

I believe that every moment in existence is in fact not "ours" each moment belongs to the fabric of the universe, and we are a part of the Universal Dance, we are as harmonious as our ability to let go and wonder permits. And this poem attempts to capture that feeling.

Be The Moment

Can you please tell me why you are running?
"The day is running away from me!"
So life is running away from you?
"Yes!"..
because each moment is so precious,
and we are running everyday,
because we feel we must... provide....
must... have this,
I have to be this, I have to, I have to...
And the anxiety of being,
living worshiping the roll of time,
preoccupying yourself with it to the point of fervor,
and nothing is ever as good as it could be if you had this,
or if you could afford this.....

And then one day you are walking home
and you find that old alley way:
the one you used to run and play in as a child,
it is almost the end of the day.

The breeze wafts the smell of lilac past you,
and the sound of children playing at the neighbors
is round and full of meaning in your heart.

Your feet tread gently along,
more and more slowly
and you see a flock of pigeons leave their roost
on the graying roof next door.

Suddenly time seems to stand still
and you notice 'light' for the first time
...maybe... the incredible impermanence
of everything around you, everything...
and how at any moment you could be gone...

And the delicious warmth of the sun on your back
seeps into you
and the weight of the bags in your hands
seem to inform you that you are learning.
And everything beams in on you,
like a great smile that reaches
from every corner of the moment,
and you laugh:
a laugh that is released as easily
as clear water gushes from a spring......
You are that spring,
and the moment is always here..
so BE IT.

In Total Trust

by Andreja Cepus

In a moment when you choose to answer your Soul Call and you let go of all the old structures of your life, a Trust comes in: A trust to your own self. A trust to your Soul, because she knows and you don't. In order to follow her guidance and let the magic in, no compromises are possible. You have to be All. You have to have a total trust.

In Total Trust

In total trust I am sailing
With the winds of New Dawn
Not knowing the destination
Not knowing the way
In total trust I am sailing
With the waves of one ocean
Through portals of dimensions
Through sunny days and starry nights
With the Wind in my hair
With sparkle in my eyes
In the Now moment.
In total trust.

Just Dare

by Shiloh Sophia McCloud

Poetry and painting are devotional acts to me, a spiritual practices, prayers and ways to share my love. My creations are the bountiful harvest from a life lived in service to Beauty and the Divine. I feel like a tree whose branches offer fruits and flowers to the sky – that must be –because they do not belong to me. My creations are both my offering and my overflow.

When I create with inquiry and intention, I am able to open a door to the sacred space between worlds. That is where I paint from – straddling spirit and matter, unmanifest and manifest, broken dreams and dreams fulfilled, suffering and healing. It is here that I find I can synchronize my own heartbeat with that of the world. Where I am in some small way one with all that is, even just for a few moments. But first, I have to dare to be.

Just Dare

Dare to re-invent yourself
when you don't know what that looks like yet.

Dare to dream bigger than
you feel comfortable dreaming.

Dare to love unreasonably,
even if you have been hurt.

Dare to practice radical self love
even when you aren't sure how.

Dare to practice big compassionate love
for others, even those you don't know.

Dare to say yes to your own self
when family or friends don't understand anymore.

Dare to not let fear get in your way,
and when it does, dare to keep moving.

Dare to be the most you that you can be
while accepting yourself right as you are.

Dare to discover what beautiful means,
to you and only you.

Dare to call yourself an artist, a poet,
a dreamer, a thinker, a revolutionary.

Dare to take passionate action
so that your fire will be lit within you.

Dare to take risks that make you feel hopeful
when you don't know how it will all work.

Dare to be a colorful being, and dance alone.
Dare to live. Dare to love. Dare to laugh.

Dare to not get it right. Dare to get back up.
Dare to live in amazing grace.

Over the Horizon

by Ruth Calder Murphy

As with so many poems, this one is the reflection of a flash of realization. Not a realization that fear holds me back, but the realization that I can choose to step beyond fear. It's a simple realization, really - the old truth that we only live fully when we leave our comfort zones... And yet, it presented itself in this new way: "Everything worth having lies on the other side of fear". It's not that there's no more fear, but that fear is, in many ways, like a horizon - a line that can be crossed.

As with all horizons, when it is crossed, a new one forms. This is a good thing - to keep on travelling, pushing forward. Not to stop because we've crossed a line, but to feel the achievement, recover and replenish... Then, aim for the next.

Every so often, the horizon disappears because, in our running for it, we suddenly realize that we're flying and the world spreads out beneath us, limitless... And that is when we glimpse the potential of life beyond fear. Mostly, though, we run - or walk, or crawl - but the exhilaration is the same when we are able to look back and see how far we've come.

Over The Horizon

It calls me -
Something Wonderful,
Something Divine...
The Everything
that pulls at my heart and
hangs,
ripe and golden in the spaces
between thoughts...
It calls
from across the line,
over the horizon,
beyond Fear.
Bold and free,
a new Me,
I step,
strong -
the bars breaking
that were holding,
restraining -
and so I fly.
Way up high,
the horizon expands -
no more lines,
no more limits -
becoming oceans
and verdant lands,
mountains and valleys,
green forests
and golden sands.
Everything that calls my name
is here -
across the line,
over the horizon,
beyond fear.

Open Lotus

by Jennieke Janaki

I wrote this poem to encourage the feeling of giving oneself completely and without fear. By opening oneself as we as women are intended, we make sure that we flower, and thus express the highest potential of love and wisdom.

Only when we have the courage to open all the way, can we receive the full spectrum of the Truth. We as women have the innate capacity of surrender to become the vessel of Divine Will.

Open Lotus

My beautiful blossoming flower
Your colors magnificent
A delicate perfume
You are an exquisite artist
Your ability to shine is enlightening
When your petals open in the early morning
Still covered with fresh raindrops
Fragile and so vulnerable
I will take care of you
In your openness
Full of wisdom
Strong and fertile
I unite with my blossoming Soul
Be the pure Lotus flower
That I made you to be
I will shower you with all my Divine Virtues.

Reflection

by Kiernan Antares

S o many of us long to be held steady in the heart of the Divine, and serve in the world as a beacon of light. We ask and ask for direction; *what is my purpose, who am I, how can I serve?* All the while knowing where our heart guides us, yet the truth of it doesn't fully integrate into our *beingness* somehow: we hold back, we doubt, we don't fully understand.

This poem is about a moment of reflection when it suddenly does, and in that moment we are free to be all that we are.

Reflection

I gaze into the waters of life
in the morning after
the darkest night
and there
the flame ignites

The Divine Spark
filling the dark caverns
of my soul

Burning away the questions
of a lifetime pondering
and suddenly
I knew
I understood with certainty

Why my feet walk upon the Earth
why my Spirit beckons

With an elusive surety
now secure
I am she

The flame within.

Her Little and Bigger Self
by Krista Katrovas

T his poem came out of a meditation on my yoga practice, and how
vital it is to embrace the fullness of our being.

Her Little and Bigger Self

She is a wolf, not a downward facing dog.
She is an eagle, not a pigeon.
She is a tiger, not a cat.
Though she doesn't look down
upon the smaller versions of herself
because deep within she knows
she's all of them,
and that some days,
she is a downward facing dog, not a wolf.
She is a pigeon, not an eagle.
She is a cat, not a tiger.
Her teachers taught her
how to embrace the full spectrum,
of what it means to be both
her little and bigger self,
and she is learning.
Learning how to keep her head
high in the heavens,
her feet rooted in the dirt,

bringing heaven to hell
earth to sky
each time she unrolls
her mat.

This is Love

by Carolyn Riker

At the moment of writing I was thinking of gratitude, which is a word with multiple entities. As I listed what I was truly grateful for, I felt love like I've never felt before.

What triggers my emotions? I can hardly begin to define. I will see a flower, hear a bird, feel a smile, touch into music and viola! Something mystical happens. I'm transported through clouds and wind and what flows out happens to be words.

Love is elusive and difficult to translate. The love I try to express in this poem is multidimensional and permeates the soul. It's an unconditional love where one can feel safe. It is as expansive as it is real. As we open to this universal love, we are connected as one.

Imagine all the stars touching each other. We are but a speck in infinity. We are the stars, the filaments that tether this love. I'm enraptured and humbled by this cosmic concept. It brings me to my knees and fills me in more ways than I can say. Therefore, I realize this is something I must share. I send love through this poem and pray it will find you and touch the corners of your heart.

This is Love

I will hold this mystical moment.
I will tenderly stroke the words with my virtual pen
I will tease the wispy tendrils
That rise from within
The dots connect to the stars of my heart

I will reach into the core of my soul,
To translate an unspoken language
I feel the words sing.

Incense burns clarity in the cornerless chambers of my heart.
Music and movement express the pauses of beginning and end.

She shares what has been heard,
A lineage passed through a sea of thoughts

It is love:
        shapeless,
                timeless,
                        universal.

Birds sing,
        after a storm
Trees sway,
        to the cascading vibrations
The ground breathes,
        to unite our hearts
Stars pulsate, as we give birth
        to answers we seek.

I dance with my heart as I breathe.
I hear the lyrical hum of mother earth.
I bend to the folds of nature's arms,
as she wraps warmth around my soul.

This is love.

Cradle your darkness in your arms
Embrace the hidden opportunities
As the shadows reveal the light.

Jenn Grosso

4

Darkness

We have always been mystified by darkness. Humankind's enchantment with the expansive night skies, have even caused us to project detailed narratives of our own lives into the stars. From astronomy to astrology, we reach into the black universe in search of ourselves, seeing symbols of our own psyches and futures orbiting in the cosmos. It's as if our DNA were programmed to do so: to reach *outward* in search of keys that unlock what dwells *within*.

Poetic hearts explore their own dark, inner galaxies with as much intrigue as Galileo pointed his telescope at the beautiful night skies, for we have a sense that, ultimately, there may not be much difference between the two. As we embark on expeditions into the microcosm of creative forces, we become pioneers of infinite fields of imagination that -like the stars- become only visible to us only during our darkest nights. Consequently, many of our poems are grown in the dark womb of our beings, and their emergence is never without pain.

Pain seems to pull poetry from places in us we never knew existed before. In darkness we dance with our demons and duel with our doubts, while flirting with the unknown, the unexamined, the inexplicable and even, the places we fear. Like burning meteorites, we feel the obsolete parts of ourselves falling away in achy blazes of extermination. Unsure of whether to hold on or let go, the poet injects meaningfulness into the destruction, birthing beauty from chaos, even in the midst of utter discomfort.

Emily Dickinson wrote about darkness as something a poet eventually becomes accustomed to, and even craves at times, like a longing to hear musical notes played in the minor key. For we feel the interconnectedness between opposing energies in the universe, like trees that draw their nourishment from dark soils. Sensitive to these energies, we intuit that the brightest lights cast the darkest shadows.

The tight and restrictive cases of our former conceptions of reality must crack, before wider perspectives emerge. Sometimes we lose ourselves in the shattered shells, and rummage amongst the scattered debris for any remnants of the person we once thought we were. Ironically, the loss of stability seems to function as a catalyst for deep insights and rejuvenated views. In yielding to the dark winter of our hearts, we allow for the seeds of our spring seasons to germinate.

In the following pages, we become intimate witnesses to the deepest, darkest struggles of poetic hearts, as they take brave dives into the most uncomfortable parts of their beings. We hear the women describe themselves as unraveling, dissolving, desperate to escape and being swallowed whole by quicksand. They shatter under avalanches of fears and relived traumas. Yet even as they unveil intolerable grief, withering hopes and unspeakable agony, in surrendering to the darkness, they create a brighter existence for themselves. Making brokenness unexpectedly beautiful, these poets inject value into their struggles, certain of their need of the night to see the stars.

Quicksand

by Ruth Calder Murphy

This poem is about life and death, exhilaration and depression. I wrote it quite a few years ago and it is, in many ways, a sort of autobiography: A reflection of how, if I stop and listen, I hear the sound of Time, marching. And it is my own footsteps I hear, echoing through the years, from physical birth to physical death, my own footsteps, carving out new roads, new journeys, across my soul.

I've written happier - ecstatic, celebratory - poems about this journey and these 'deep' moments. "Quicksand", however, represents the no less valid times when the darkness descends and all I can do is listen to the footsteps, and try to keep on breathing, when to struggle is to sink and I just have to hope that my feet will find solid ground before the quicksand swallows me completely.

We all have our own versions of quicksand in our lives. This quicksand, too, is a part of the journey to be embraced and valued. These times are precious, too. We need the night to see the stars and, having survived the darkness, we move forward into a more brilliant dawn as a result.

This poem is for all my spiritual siblings who know the darkness well, and who feel the pull of the quicksand. It comes with hope. We will survive.

Quicksand

Again I hear my footsteps
upon my silent soul
that echo to eternity
and tread from pole to pole.
They chart my every movement
from bloodshed at my birth
to that sequestered moment
when my dust returns to earth.
They pulse through all the seasons,
they thunder in my thought
and rhythmic send my throbbing heart
to where its life was wrought.
When suddenly the silence
engulfs me like a sea.
I slip into the sinking sand
that slowly swallows me.

I Want To Run
by Vrinda Aguilera

My poem is about growth and the discomfort that can accompany it. Often when I write, I'm not totally clear what's going to come out and when it does it's often a little or a lot different than what I started out with. But that's part of the fun!

I am still formulating this poem and trying to understand it. Of course, that is part of my process and what it facilitates is exactly that: exploring and understanding myself. This exploration is continuous. This is but one glimpse into my evolutionary trail.

I Want To Run

I do not like this feeling of itchiness,
I do not like this sensation of discomfort,
discontent
Right now I am not comfortable in my own skin, in my own house,
    relationships, or LIFE

I writhe
I seethe
I am irate
Irrational

I WANT TO RUN!
My trigger is that of a hare's,
Ready to spring at the slightest provocation or tremor.
To bound away at lightening speed,
Scrabbling in place for the merest of milliseconds until I am gone,
Jettisoned off into the desert screen.
Now you see me, now you don't.
Blinded by a spray cloud of dust,
You are left spitting out harsh sand and gritty pebbles.
My frantic, powerful jackrabbit kicks
Stir up a billowing smokescreen.
That is how I would like it, at least.
For then I would be safe,
Invisible,
A quickly receding dot in the distance,
Camouflaged by the arid, drab landscape.

Gone.

I WANT TO HIDE!
I writhe and itch
I am like a lizard or snake, discomfited in my own skin
Ready to shed I scrape myself roughly against sharp edges
With my words,
Actions.
Looking for relief, I strike out blindly against those I love.
My need makes me abandon the desire for the softness of comfort
    and healing balms.
I don't want soothing or healing
I am driven by a force that begs for cataclysmic rupture.

The encasement of my very self, once so warm and cozy
Is now a binding, suffocating girdle of sorts.
It doesn't fit.
Driven by a force larger than myself,
Guided by the invisible hands of spirit, instinct.
As a snake sheds its old skin, leaving behind a perfect replica of its
    former self,
So do I yearn to emulate this reptilian way.

I slide seamlessly towards the dense, green underbrush.
In my new skin I will be tender and vulnerable.
Glance away with inattention for even a second,
you will be left wondering if I was here at all
The empty shell of my discarded self
The only proof of my passing through.
Under a sheltering crack in a boulder,
I hide.

Hope Took A Hike

by Edith Lazenby

Sometime life gives us challenges. Sometimes the challenge is finding the value in life. There are always curve balls and the unexpected. Yet when the floor is pulled out, when I am left questioning all I have known, hope takes a hike...and this is where it took me.

Hope Took A Hike

Hope took a hike
down a trail and
I cannot see where
she is going: lost
I seek her footprints;
Eyes bent toward branches
and try to find her scent.

I fear she left me here
in a wood with trees
and fallen limbs
on a night without
benefit of the moon.

I collect the wood
and begin a fire
though it is summer.
The air feeds the flames.
I want to burn like that.
I want to feel passion
ignite my insides with meaning.

Instead I left care in a door
I can no longer open.
Time is a mist in my mind.

Nothing holds nothing.
I look inside to find a shadow.
If there is a shadow, there
must be a light to feed me.

Yet darkness swallows
my feet up to my head.
My eyes won't close.
Need becomes a cosmetic
like lipstick that never stays
and I never find the right shade.

Unraveling

by Melissa June

'Unraveling' is a poem I wrote inspired by string. This poem is about my mistakenly seeing myself as an emotionally weak woman with a lot of troubles in life. So I released myself on a downward journey, unraveling, to set myself free. And I finally landed as no longer weak, but strong!

Unraveling

I am torn, mangled thread
shreds entwined, firmly into a ball
tears of rough fiber discolored red
as I am cut, beginning to fall

Extracting the needle from within
bleeding, to unravel all my pain
I untangle, breaking off as I spin
decimated thread, with sorrow's stain

Ravaged strands, fell to be free
my weak twine, now unwound
the knot of darkness once held me
though no longer has me bound

The despair that pained me clears
my heart's released from the sling
threads grew strong, dry of tears
I land, as unbreakable string.

Be Brave

by Maureen Kwiat Meshenberg

I find my courage even in my deepest fear. I step forward when my heart cries to hold back. Stepping onto an unseen path, but moving my feet forward, my soul calls me to be brave.

We all meet these crossings in our lives, when we feel like falling to the ground and staying there, but we stand up and rise and be brave. From the depths of our beings, even when fear tries to paralyze us, we find our bravery deep within us, it calls to us, in our darkest moments.

Be Brave

Be Brave...
oh soul of mine-
when shadows consume
your seeking,
when darkness covers your way-
your flickering that comes
from your glowing
will light the way.
Be Brave...
even when your foot
slips against rock-

even if you fall on your hands,
touching cold ground-
lift up, and be brave.
Your courage is your surrendering,
rising and reaching,
even when you feel
you can't anymore.
Be brave...
for the colors of life
hold you-
the brightness that you are
consoles you.
as the love of the Divine keeps you,
whispers to you,
Be Brave.

Beloved Struggle

by Aisha Wolfe

A woman found a cocoon. One day a small opening appeared, she sat and watched the butterfly for several hours as it struggled to force its body through the little hole. Then it seemed to stop making any progress. It appeared stuck!

The woman decided to help the butterfly and with a pair of scissors she cut open the cocoon. The butterfly then emerged easily, but something was odd: The butterfly had a swollen body and shriveled wings. The woman watched the butterfly expecting it to take on its correct proportions. But nothing changed. The butterfly stayed the same. It was never able to fly.

In her kindness and haste, the woman did not realize that the butterfly's struggle to get through the small opening of the cocoon is nature's way of forcing fluid from the body of the butterfly into its wings so that it would be ready for flight.

As butterflies need to work hard to emerge fit from their cocoons, we all need life's struggles to make us strong. This poem is about our relationships to such struggles in our lives, and learning to see them as grace.

Beloved Struggle

You struggle because there is a payoff
You struggle with struggle because
when you're not in struggle, what is there?

When you don't know what is there
Then you don't know who you are
When you don't know who you are
You won't know how to live

There is a way to live in the state of unknown
It is to flow

You don't need to know
To flow
You don't need to learn to let go
To flow

Letting go is a natural happening
When you stop avoiding
Whatever it is you fear the most

What you fear the most is waiting for you
In the direction you most resist going

Down

If you are miserable
How miserable can you be?

If you are stuck
How entangled can you get?

If you are alone
How far down the secret ladder can you go?

Find out what you are miserable about
And marry it

Make love with it
Day in, day out.

Until you no longer fear its tone
Until you can no longer look into its face

And not see Grace

Surrender

by Carolyn Riker

Life doesn't always arrive as a neat package. It often shows up with rough and unraveling edges especially after it travels along winding decades of experience. The wrapping paper loses its luster and the twine becomes frayed. The heaviness of the package gets overwhelming at times: the responsibility to find its vision and destination daunting.

On a summer afternoon, I lay on the sandy colored carpet like a starfish at low tide. I had nothing left to give and my heart was shockingly exposed. My feet touched a pile of laundry and my hands grazed a stack of papers. Then, I closed my eyes and surrendered.

I settled into my breathing and asked for guidance. I could hear what seemed like ocean waves lapping gently along a shore. Within minutes, a soft summer rain began to fall. Rain was not in the forecast but it came anyway. It was one of those universal messages that showered me with peacefulness. It gracefully washed over my confusion as I let the clutter in my mind melt into the synthetic fibers, imagining a beach. That evening, after rearranging some furniture in my heart and home, I settled into a new writing place and wrote this poem.

Surrender

On this summer's eve,
set your intentions wide
I can see you hold the Sun and the Moon
A heavy juxtaposition
Close your eyes.
Linger long as you caress the foliage
and sip delicate rose water
Listen to the trees as they whisper wisdom:
Breathe, bend and lift
Chant with the owls
Let the light of the Moon guide your inner flame
Sail the turbulent seas of the North and South nodes.
Drink the alabaster nectar
Let the drizzle of the rain hum a lullaby,
Surrender, now
To an elliptical hammock
Suspended between the stars
To hold and infuse your sensitive heart
As it clearly resonates with a universal Om.

Pursuing Peace
by Jessica Mokrzycki

It seems one desire common to the human condition is our desire to be happy and to find peace. We look for it everywhere and oftentimes try to fill the emptiness within with all sorts of attractive things this world offers, only to be left feeling even more dissatisfied and empty than before.

The restlessness our souls experience, I feel, is a symptom of our natural longing to connect to God and realize our true natures. For those of us who pursue truth and understanding into the reality of God, and our eternal natures, the journey we embark on can be laden with lush forests offering fruits heavy with refreshing eternal nectar.

But the landscape can also become barren and dry, as well as tumultuous and unsteady, causing our hearts to be uncertain of what the truth really is. Making us doubt ourselves, and even the existence of God. In our searching we can enter into what the mystics call "The Dark Night of the Soul".

The following poem reflects my internal struggle to make sense of things spiritually. It shows glimpses of my doubts and the distress that can be felt when one realizes that much of this material existence is full of suffering.

The poem also speaks of my mantra, the *maha-mantra*, which has become like an anchor to me: keeping me from being washed off course completely, birthing peace and hope within my heart, offering me refuge.

Pursuing Peace

When all hope drains away
and all that is left is filth and decay;
When longing is all that the heart feels
The soul reaching out for something to heal,
The pain that reaches deeper than eternity
All that meets one's agonizing pleas
Is an emptiness vast as the ocean is wide
The seed of light long buried deep inside
covered with thick layers of maya and grief
One's spirit longing for much needed reprieve.
This life seems a tragic and laughable dance
Poised on the pinnacle of misery and chance,
Like a wave joy rises only to meet sorrow
The light of today kisses the darkness of tomorrow.
Is there a God out there to sweep me away
from the tragedies life throws my way?
Or is it all just a jumble of happenstance
No meaning except for this moment, no God to glance
up from His undoubtedly busy duties of creating

to, in His mercy, absorb up some of this pain permeating
My soul making it throb and quiver,
Making my heart so cold that it ceases even to shiver.
Maybe there is no way to truly find out the mysteries that hold
All of mankind in suspense, a story truly untold.
We can speculate and forecast our fates
But none really knows what is scribbled on reality's slate.
All that I know is when the darkness settles in
I repeat the Holy Names as if they were a holy hymn.
In them my heart takes refuge and searches for peace
Waiting for the storm's raging winds to finally cease.

Death's Song

by Jenn Grosso

For those days that seem darker than dark, remember this too shall pass. There are always new beginnings at every turn. Or as Carl Jung used to say: "There is no coming to consciousness without pain."

Death's Song

In the bleak and the despair
Hold on tightly to yourself
Be comforted by Death's Song.

These cycles they come and go
Every day in every minute
Another moment's death.

Breathe and take it all in
The just beginnings
And all their many endings.

Nothing stays forever

Change is the only constant
Hold on tightly to yourself.

Cradle your darkness in your arms
Embrace the hidden opportunities
As the shadows reveal the light.

With every little death
Newfound joy in the beginning
Another moment is born.

Grief

by Edith Lazenby

Sadness is always close to me. One of my teachers told me my beauty rests in how I hold my sadness because it is so much a part of me.

And yet even more so today, years later, I find what holds me is the grace I find within the poem: the way I can graze what aches in my heart and yet find its release in my hands, as if each prayer held a bird learning to flap its wings and as my hands open, take flight.

Grief

Like a cricket's legs, sadness
Waxes on the wings
On my back few can see
As they are rays
Of light holding shadows
As if shade from a tree
Where I find quiet, a reprieve
From the steps
To keep this dance, my life,
Moving to music

Each tear makes, like rain
On a roof, drops paddling
On a summer day so
A breeze can come, taking
The heaviness of heat,
The weight of a nameless angst
That holds each foot
Rooted to the earth, feeding
Self as I ground down
To pull the energy into my heart
Where love is a promise,
Roses out my window, stars
In the sky, the kitten in my hand,
Change folds its prayer
From there, to here and back,
Able to touch, from anywhere.

I Saw You There

by Maureen Kwiat Meshenberg

Sometimes, there are no words you can offer, no comforting advice you can give to someone who is so dear to you, going through a tremendous ache in their life. Sometimes, it is more comforting to offer your tears, your silence, your tender listening; just letting them, know you are there for them with an open heart.

I Saw You There

I saw you,
there-
hands to face,
tears that-
spilled upon,
your day.

you held them close,
not wanting-
anyone to see,
I reached with-
my hand,
my tears,
covering yours-
I did not offer,
words like-
it will be okay,
it will be alright,
sound so empty sometimes,
even contrite.
let the eyes of my soul,
give you my listening-
with ears of the heart,
open and true.
without words that compromise,
this moment of holding-
giving you a resting place,
embraced in love and grace,
for you.

Dreams

by Sandra Allagapen

I wrote this poem after working with someone who felt like a failure because she hadn't achieved one of her childhood dreams. It didn't matter that she had already achieved so much. She still judged herself and her life by the things she hadn't done and therefore no matter how good her life got, it was never enough to chase away her sadness and her regrets. It saddened me that she found more value in dwelling in the past than in creating a future where she was fulfilled.

The main message of this poem is that sometimes the dream isn't the destination; sometimes it's just a signpost to the direction we needed to take. If we make the choice to replace regrets with the faith that all is indeed well, then we will be able to be fully present in our lives, enjoy all the good that is already there, and focus on the future we want for ourselves. And today, this is my prayer for all of us.

Dreams

A face in the mirror
A stranger yet familiar
From the depths of her soul
A story insisting on being told
Of a girl once full of hope
That great things in her life will unfold

Thirty years have passed
Some dreams just did not last
Only her eyes tell the tale
Of a spirit once certain to prevail
Who now mourns dreams long gone
And all the things left undone

She wants to hide
But the face in the mirror holds tight
The keeper of her soul
She won't rest until she's whole
Patiently she waits
A world of compassion in her gaze

It's ok, she whispers
Let them go, she encourages
Those broken dreams you shoulder
Are no longer yours to cry over
Some had no purpose
Others were just signposts

It's time to surrender

And make space for the future
Regrets make lousy companions
What you need is passion
The future is yet to come
Who says it can't be awesome

A spark of inspiration
Can lead to the greatest creation
Paving the way for new beginnings
That you can't yet imagine
Because to catch a moonbeam
You have to dream new dreams.

Oh, Insecure Self, Why Do You Visit?

by Carolyn Riker

This life doesn't make sense and it doesn't come with a manual. I learn through falling hard. Lessons that I thought I learned still swim to the surface of an endless pool. In this poem, insecurity ripples her familiar state of fear and doubt. There's a convergence of feelings and a disconnect with reality.

I learn the most when I'm at my lowest. When I let go of what-will-everyone-think? I find that it doesn't matter, what they think. Redefining the self in terms of accepting who am, what I stand for and believe in, are all within. Spiritually, I find I'm intertwined with a greater force and an intricate part of an endless universe. The ripples I see are my own illusions of how I should be or what I've been told to be. The tapes in my memory are being rewritten and my DNA is being rewired.

I am love, compassion, sadness, rage and joy. These are all aspects of me and it's okay to feel and express them. Insecurity tugs at my heart like a child whose hand wasn't held long enough. Now I can reach in and hold that child's insecurity, let her know it's okay, that she's loved as I reach the other hand to the universe.

Oh, Insecure Self, Why Do You Visit?

Why do you surface at such ridiculous times?
>Letting doubt sneak in.
>Another window has opened.
>I can feel the wind through my heart.

Where did you come from?
Why are you here?
>It's me, the real you, from inside.
>You hold on, afraid to let go
>of what you protected for so long.

I am impatient with this moment....I try to flee
From the lurking, churning, gnawing:
>It resides in my core.
>It lodges in my heart.
>I can't breathe.

Everything seems wrong.
My decision and thoughts are muddled.
Challenging what I believe.
Doubt creeps in...The floor slips away.
What's there to hold onto, when everything seems unreal?
A child's voice capitulates, a woman's heart,
>Protect me. It's all that you've known.

Oh insecure self why are you here again?
What lessons do you bring?
Why do you seem mightier when I get closer to me?

A woman's voice whispers, her wisdom dips inward.
>Sit with the rise and fall and let insecurity and fear visit.
>It's something to notice rather than run or push aside.
>It will keep persisting until you don't hide.

Stillness won't come when you continue to fight.
Therefore, embrace it and acknowledge:
Change is different.
The unknown is unclear.
The future is blurry.

Stay here in this moment.
The past is gone, the future is not.
It's only now.

Stay still and breathe with whatever
Each feeling that washes over,
Know you will not drown.
The water is an illusion yet swims in your eyes.
Rain falls up. Rules fall away.
Release the fist that bruised and scarred the core.
Embrace the self that was never allowed to be.
Let the woman enter in, with love
Let insecurity go, with no regret
Let it all swirl out to sea...
For in this moment,
just breathe.

Slumberland

by Mariann Martland

For longer than I can remember sleep, real life-giving sleep, has been elusive in my life. I have been plagued by a series of nightmares, night terrors and other equally disturbing nighttime problems since I was a little girl. In the last year or two I have begun to link this to early childhood trauma and a part of what I have now acknowledged to be post traumatic stress disorder.

As I have been working through the process of recovering memories; processing the abuse, the loss and the health implications, and using everything I have in discovering my true self, a good night's sleep has been an increasingly rare occurrence. This is in spite of my practices of meditation, keeping mindful and breathing through this painful process.

Often, as I battle and try to reconcile myself with my sleepless nights, I write. Writing has become like breathing for me as I attempt to find, accept and express my story...my truth. These words came to me at 5am on a dark, windy winter's morning after some intense weeks of flashbacks and discoveries new details about my childhood. I called out in my exhausted, yet ever alert state, asking the universe to allow me to sink into an undisturbed, peaceful sleep.

Slumberland

Grant me the gift of space to sleep, softly,
To sink into the sweet sounds of Slumberland;
Lying within the lilting lullaby,
Hearing hope replace horror.
Give me time to be calmly cradled into morning
With real, renewed strength to stand, tall
To face the fire of the ferocious sun,
Who highlights the heartaches of a heavy day.
Allow me to reclaim my restoration,
To feel free to open my falling eyes, widely
Without extended exhaustion from the demons of the dark.
Show me how to step into silent stillness;
To bask in the beginnings of this revelation,
Learning to dance within the deep delight of dreams.
Teach me to trust in the temptation of surrender.
To concede control to the security of the stars;
To let go of my weighted worries to the whispers, who
Recall my resolve to release my mind to relaxation.
Lead me with the lingering light of the moon
To a land where I can slide into slow, safe sleep.

Shards

by Ruth Calder Murphy

I think that, to anyone who's been through the darkness, this poem speaks for itself. For the darkness is real. It's tangible, it hurts and it can destroy.

Knowing that these times can lead to a greater appreciation of the other times – knowing that they can make us better, stronger, more radiant – doesn't necessarily make a scrap of difference when the darkness descends. In fact, everything we once knew has a habit of disappearing into that darkness and being swallowed whole.

But when even the slightest glimmer, the tiniest pinprick of light, penetrates the pitch that sticks to our soul and stops our eyes, when the stars begin to come out, it's sometimes possible to catch a glimpse of this: We need the night to see the stars and, whilst being smashed to shards again and again hurts like crazy, every time, the shards reflect more brightness, and every crack lets in - and out - more light.

Shards

Whilst journeying along the path of dreams,
or flying high on Summer's gentle breath,
I've sometimes, frequently, it often seems,
been flung to Earth with all the force of Death,
My spirit torn to tattered, bloody strings,
reflected in the shards of broken soul
that lie around me, glinting, dangerous things,
each one an echo of a shining whole
And every time, I gather to my heart
the pieces that are every part of me
and step once more into another Start,
another path, another flying free
and every time, the shards reflect more bright
and every crack lets in - and out - more light.

Sometimes, so to reach the rainbowed core,
the pulsing heart where life is at its best,
the rest must first be flayed and opened, raw,
the naked treasure flowing from its chest.
And so with shards of my own soul, I cleave,
and paring bone from marrow, mind from thought,

undress myself and then, ethereal, leave
to journey to the place where life is wrought
And gather, as I go along my way,
new flesh, new thoughts, new ways of being me,
new music in my ears, new games to play,
new ways to fly, new freedom just to be
and all the pain of paring, still I bear
and know that when I feel it, life is there.

The Air Finds It Hard To Breathe

by Jenn Grosso

"Poetry is what happens when nothing
else can." ~Charles Bukowski

In some of our darkest moments, that's all we can do. Breathe and write. We can then regain our footing and become stronger through that experience. Even though we might be temporarily lost, we reconnect within ourselves by putting pen to paper and just breathing. Finding that inner sanctuary of stillness we can make ourselves whole once more. This poem is one of those fleeting moments of darkness when poetry was what happened when nothing else could.

The Air Finds It Hard To Breathe

Thick and arduous, my breath is stifled
I stop dead in my tracks and gasp for sustenance
My head spins and chest tightens.

I am doubting myself again, every last part
In this process I cut myself into little pieces
Putting it all under the microscope and peering through.

It all looks so ugly, isolated there in front of me
In the darkness I forget the beauty of the whole
This forgetting is a slippery slope and my light diminishes.

Tightness and panic, I struggle to inhale
My breathing quickens and my muscles tense up
I am here once again in desolate self-hesitation.

I discredit my achievements and victories
In this place they no longer hold meaning
The spotlight turns onto the failures and defeats.

I override my confidence and self-assurance
Degrading my self-worth, beauty seeps through my fingers
I am unable to get a hold onto anything.

My mind becomes the trickster, twisting and contorting
Every second takes me ten steps backwards
Revealing the transgressions behind the mask.

This colorless landscape terrifies me and I recoil
I know there is a better way, a happier path awaiting me
If I so choose to rise above the bleak and barren.

I take a breath, and slowly take another coming back into myself
I am so much more than my fears and wounds
In my arms I cradle all these broken pieces holding them tight.

Welcome to my curse, my moment of inner collapse
Restoring myself I fasten the parts together once more
Take another deep breath and turn the light back on.

Shadows and Saturn

by Carolyn Riker

I wrote this poem during an intense moment of just plain, mind-numbing, painful insight. Life is full of transitions. As I learn about myself through yoga, meditation and Vedic Astrology, I have to focus on the universal story being told.

Change and understanding come into our lives for a reason. It allows us to see what we don't want to see and what we need to see. It serves to release what no longer resonates in my heart as I learn to let go.

As my heart breaks, new light and love pours in. Letting go is different from giving in or giving up. It's not about being broken or re-traumatizing our self. It's about freedom from the preconceived self. Finding the real self is liberating.

Shadows and Saturn

Who I thought I was
    I am not.
Saturn steady, determined, searing
    Heart hurts
    Ego crushed
Piercing the reality that isn't
Staying in limbo?
    Not a choice.
Moving forward?
    Necessary
Memories surface
    See them as memories
    Let go of who created them
The false self
    Hides the true self
    It will take time to find her
Hitting a low
Raking over the bones

Crushed
This is an opportunity!
Seems bizarre
Head swims in grief
Staying with the moments
The painful notes crescendo
The waves of realizing
It doesn't serve you any longer
Hiding in the walls
That hides the soul
Truth cuts to the core
The shadows speak and tunnel deep
Whether awake or asleep
The shadows of my soul exposed
I ache
Pushing me through a heart
Every piece is strained
It's got my attention
Doubts and questions fall at sharp angles
Sitting still,
the moment quiet
The lonely, humming sounds of nothingness
I shake
The core of me dead
I have nowhere else to go
I haven't failed.
Finally, *I surrender.*

Let Today Be A New Day

by Maureen Kwiat Meshenberg

My mind has a way of pulling up my past. It wants me to relive sorrows, broken stories that fracture my living. This poem reflects my consciousness coming to its breath, and allowing the newness of each day to hold me, just as I am.

Let Today Be A New Day

regret came to my doorway,
even when I wanted-
to let the dwelling of such presence,
steal my day...
I said, be on your way.
when my past came with,
it's haunting,
instead of compassionate recalling-
my mind slipped behind,
my breath and whispered...
be on your way.
when life hits hard,
avalanche of fears-
I say with tender tears,
let them fall on me-
like petals from my heart's garden,
blowing on a gentle breeze-
through my soul.
I hold myself and say,
let today be a new day.

We delight in the beauty of the butterfly,
but rarely admit the changes it has gone through
to achieve that beauty.

Maya Angelou

5

Transformation

Life sweeps us, and everything around us, into a dance with time that magically transforms everything it touches. From the tiny atoms that make up our bodies, to the enormous planets orbiting in space, the universe swirls like one endless alchemical process, leaving nothing, or no one, behind. This cosmic choreography animates everything with an unstoppable evolutionary drive that draws from the infinite, inviting us to extend our existence into eternity.

Magnificent movement is at the core of all life, and it beckons our participation so that we not become complacent. It pulls us out of stagnation and challenges us to creatively reinvent ourselves with each cycle of creation and destruction, growth and decay, darkness and light, over and over again. Perhaps, encoded in these cycles, is the message that we aren't as limited as we think we are; we aren't as finite. Constantly being stretched to entertain new perimeters of being, when we resist change, we unwittingly resist the flow of life itself.

Changes most often catapult us into stress when they involve loss, and we cling to what is being taken away from us. Yet in clenching the seeds in our palm, we deprive them of the nourishment that will turn them into trees. Like soil to seeds, the burning fires of life's alchemical forces become food for our shining souls. This is the ultimate vision of poetic hearts, as they surrender themselves to the dynamic nature of existence, however initially difficult that may be. For, in the transformation of energies, nothing is ever really lost.

From the caves of antiquity, we have always linked fire with mystical transformative forces. Though fire consumes, it also gives. This powerful paradox has weaved its way into our world's most celebrated myths, casting fire as that which transforms ordinary sight into divine vision, and as a powerful symbol of our free will. When faced with life's changes do we allow them to consume us, or invigorate us? Do we regard the changes life sets before us as detracting from our lives, or adding to them? Rather than fearing and avoiding the fire, poetic souls find ways to benefit from the light of its flames. Guided by intuition and imagination, we move through changes as we would through open doorways, making transformations our passages to healing, and growth, and new ways of being.

This chapter begins with a phoenix falling, angels speaking, fires igniting, rivers raging and a tiger pacing in her cage. The poets effortlessly squeeze juice from metaphors as they express the complexity of feelings connected with change. Here, we feel their tender hearts negotiating life's transitions in painful strokes over broad canvases, to the sound of wings being plucked, roots suffocating flowers and blood flowing. As the poets describe the ways in which life transforms them, we hear them extract lessons from regrets, become grateful for mistakes and mend wounds with meaning. Intent on thriving, instead of merely surviving, they discover resilience they never knew they had. In graceful strides these thoughtful women release blame, with the realization that everything has the potential to move us in sacred ways, if only we let it.

As the Phoenix Falls

by Jenn Grosso

Walking on the path of our own spiritual journey, we can sometimes feel like we go around in circles, always beginning. Yet in writing this poem, I was comforted with the fact that we never truly stay the same.

Reflecting on the nature of change, I believe we are always shifting ever so slightly, moving forward always transformed somehow with every step.

As the Phoenix Falls

You say you've been transformed
and that you've found your way
but how different do we really become?
One step forward sometimes ten steps back
and we find ourselves at the beginning again
Alchemy's many disguises.

Walls are closing in while you react
Keep burning through the noose
Just keep burning through the noose.

Given the chance to rise above
to transmute fear and pain
trapped and stifled by ego's demands
We move in circles and in cycles
we never really stay the same
yet never stray far away from our true nature.
Keep burning through the noose
to rise again and fall once more
to rise again.

Bringing Me to My Center
by Maureen Kwiat Meshenberg

I have been finding my way back to me. Not with how I was raised, or through traditions or religion, but through meditation and finding my true me: my light, my dark, my everything!

I am continually brought to a place of compassion and healing. It brings me again and again to that space of centering, as I shift and fold inward. Always bringing myself to the present living of me. This poem reflects this journey. May it reach and touch yours.

Bringing Me to My Center

relax oh my soul,
long enough to rest-
on your day's path with peace,
without wanting thoughts-
that wrestle with your conscious choice.
silently,
I listen to the voice-
within me,
it is my guide,
my friend,
my angel,
as it gently speaks to me,
to settle.
all that I receive-
finds the middle way,
between chaos and peace-
impermanence will never cease,
let me come to the moment-
where I am-
right now.
as it holds imperfection,
of living-
not molded by standards of this world,
but by my heart-
bringing clarity to all,
that whirls around me-
bringing me to my center.

Nature's Nectar

by Gwen Potts

This poem was written after I was shown that I still hadn't fully grasped the concept of the world as our mirror. That the world is like a huge projector screen, mirroring back to us ourselves and the things we need to learn, the gifts within all circumstances. And that it is our own selves that really create all events and circumstances, ultimately, to deepen our understanding of the Universe and our place in it.

This concept really helped me realize that although we may understand things intellectually, we continue to evolve layer by layer to an ever- higher state of consciousness. It also helped me appreciate to be kind to our selves through our 'mistakes' as without them, there would be no catalyst to grow.

Nature's Nectar

What if we took full responsibility for our own pain?
Without projecting or blaming others, realizing that when we feel
 betrayed, accused or hurt
It is simply a mirror to look at ourselves - ever deeper
That when we feel judged
We are really judging ourselves

If we realized that whatever has been 'done' to us
Is there simply as a gift to heal and release that pain
But why is it seemingly so hard to fully integrate some lessons?
We can understand them intellectually, but when they are so deeply
 carved inside
It's so much harder to let go

Some of these lessons are not even of this lifetime
But remembered by the soul
A single comment or glance into someone's eyes
A story of some bygone event etched within the soul

Its purpose to re-ignite that fire - to heal that pain
A gift to us at its deepest core
Although we are conditioned
To only see the surface event
It is only by fully feeling and expressing this pain

Can we hope to release it

Like a rose unfolding its petals with the early morning sun
Drinking in the sweet dew
That has settled on its petals
Daring to bare its centre to the shining sun - the life giver

That although it emits a great heat and energy
Provides the growth needed for the rose to blossom
Day after day it blossoms
And the bees enjoy its sweet nectar

The chain reaction of growth and evolution moves swiftly
An interconnected web each giving to the other

The rose won't blame the bee if it fails to drink its nectar
The bee won't blame the rose if its nectar isn't sweet
Each is responsible for its link in the chain
The tapestry of life

A symbiotic dance that makes the world flourish
Each understanding and accepting its part
Helping the other with no expectations

If only we as humans could learn to dance this sublime dance
Be responsible for our selves
Learn to dance together in harmony
To rejoice at the heavenly synergy we create

Just by dancing our own unique dance

The Difficulty in Forgetting
by Salyna Gracie

The events of our lives shape who we become as we navigate the rivers of our journey. Each new day presents the challenge of how we resist allowing the past to define or limit us. As we cross on stepping-stones of loss or regret, my hope is that we may we find the love and courage to live in grace.

The Difficulty in Forgetting

the past is like a river
ever-flowing currents
defying space and time

sometimes a delicate trickle
a sensation of words forgotten
always on the tip of my tongue

other days the river rages
torrents of memories flooding so fiercely
the banks of this body cannot contain it

yesterdays eddy round and round
all regret and longing
cycles that stagnate in cell and bone

today the river is restless
tempting me with its siren song
resisting the pull of things that might have been
I give thanks for this new day

A Thousand Tigers
by Ruth Calder Murphy

We are all caged, to an extent, at points in our lives: By circumstances, by other people's opinions, by wanting to fit in, by fear of the unknown. The list is probably endless – every person will have a slightly different set of things that form their "bars".

Often, our cages are comfortable and it would be easiest to simply stay inside them, using the soft, comfortable bars as pillows. Often, beyond the cage is frightening and tigers are prowling. Fears of losing other people's respect, losing one's own certainty or assurance, stepping into an unknown, outside one's comfort zone...

But the door of the cage is open and each of us has wings, if we choose to use them. That moment when I decided that my wings were stronger than the tigers, that my freedom was more valuable than the comfort: that moment I began to be free.

A Thousand Tigers

The door of my cage is open.
Will I dare
go there,
where tigers prowl?
The bars of my cage are soft.
Will they be
pillows for me
to dream of freedom?
Or will they yield to my touch,
my wings stretched wide,
fall away at the up beat
and on the down beat,
watch me rise?
My wings have the strength of a thousand tigers.
The door of my cage is open
and the world waits.

Learning To Fly

by Edith Lazenby

I wrote this poem the other night for a friend, as a gift, a way of sharing understanding of how many ways a heart can break. Like any

121

who've lived life, if lucky actually, they've known love; and then learned what they knew as love had roots in something other than compassion, giving and true care. As the Native American saying goes: "The more the heart breaks, the stronger it grows."

I find the creative process feeds the heart in all ways. A child can be the product of many things but in an ideal world, a child results because of the love of a man and a woman. Or today, same-sex partners can find a means to have a child with the love they share. Being childless, I don't have that blessing. But I do have I have writing, yoga and faith. I can lose everything else I know, but even life cannot take those three.

Learning to Fly

Feelings crack my heart
Like an egg with a chick
That's wants to peep:
Instead I see a yolk
Run with blood in the center
And though I am making
Eggs for my kids
Like I usually do, all I scramble
And beat takes my insides
Out as I toss in the butter
And begin to cook.
What's cooked and roasted
Is a spirit that wants to thrive
When instead each breath
Stops at my throat
And I chortle and choke
To find the pain of dying
Like the baby bird
That could not grow wings.
My feathers were plucked
Before they could ever fly

And I know if I could bury
What never found life,
A part that cries
Might grow wings
As I find meaning in pain
Only time can treat.
I decide to curl into a ball
And imagine a woman
Holding me as if my love
A womb able
To birth a joy
Pain won't let me know.
And as I lay in the embrace
I learn that woman is me,
And slowly a healing
Plants a seed as I find
My way to a limb
Of a tree and look up
To feel the sun warming me,
Getting ready to spread my wings.

My Heart Rises

by Carolyn Riker

Transitions are passages. Change is inevitable and with it ample opportunities are provided to grow. Each passage presents different obstacles. During times of tremendous transition, I retreat to my garden. She is patiently waiting for me and teaches me the cyclical patterns of life: quiet dormancy, budding rebirth, vibrant growth and eminent death.

The solace of nature has always been consistent and readily available with wisdom. It is one of the few places I exchange my thoughts freely as I listen to the birds, share the air with the trees, and retreat into a meditation of trust.

I wrote this poem early one morning as autumn is now nipping at the edges of my sleeves. My thoughts were quietly infused with peacefulness and her steady hand led me home.

My Heart Rises

Mist gracefully shrouds
the morning sun
fragments of dreams
still hum
a cadence of light rain
the footsteps of faeries
mystically stills my heart
enchanting prayers
offered in this sacred space
of solitude
I peacefully breathe
the cool damp air
as it teases and
dances through the trees
a playful exchange
of wind.
sunlight sees the shadows
memories cleansed
by the morning dew
a hazy world
of seeing the past
stepping into new
grateful
as I watch
my heart
rise with the sun.

Bypass Waters

by Andrea Balt

When you realize you have hands and feet and you're not really a person but an inexplicable phenomenon happening and happening and happening as we speak. And you begin to understand that all of life is improvisation, and you can't understand how your heart has not skipped one beat in all these years, and you're momentarily afraid that, now that you're pointing it out, it might suddenly stop, and you're not yet ready for that... (Never.) So here's some heart surgery in verse, to help me -- you start feeling our hands & feet again.

Bypass Waters

Be still, be still,
So I may enter in a breath,
your throat, so I can dig my way
through veins,
to that deluded heart
of yours, this way
a piece or two might be
extracted, spared,
the blood unblocked,
aortas' bail.

And all the while, hush,
be still,
the hungry hour be fed,
the stone-bread near;
the sightless ear be opened,
a drop of sound into
a deaf eye, those three words
I don't love, a substitute
of lips, the skin

no longer mute,
the beast still unconcealed.

Be still, and know man only lives
twice, once for his
poisoned heart, and yet
another
just to hear his name,
on someone else's lips.
Whose do you whisper
as you fall asleep?

And yet, be still, I say
quiet your hands,
courage is just a fine
string, not a rope.
I'm almost through, be still,
but are you sure
you want the pounding,
dear? My fatal song will do,
be still... Though you should
know: the added life
comes with a plus
of fear.

Tender Heart

by Zoe Quiney

Recently I was very touched by some simple words spoken to me "we have tender hearts". I reflected on this and it resonated deeply for me as I consider myself to be someone who leads by the heart rather than the head; which can be both a blessing and a curse. I'm learning to love my heart-lead life and all its wonderful twists and turns and the magic it can bring. So I wrote this as an ode...to my 'Tender' heart.

Tender Heart

My tender heart, it feels so much.
It fills and flows and leaps and jumps
It surges and pounds and aches and breaks
It determines decisions that I must make

My tender heart, my precious source
My sweet serenity, my deep remorse
It answers questions not yet asked
A house of truth, it wears no mask.

My tender heart, it beats and bleeds
To satisfy the soul it feeds
It loves so much, I'm sure it'll burst:
An overflowing cup, to quench infinite thirst.

My tender heart I give you peace
On days when hurt appears not to cease.
I offer you strength, a place of calm
A gentle wisdom, amid the storm.

My tender heart, please speak your truth
Your knowledge from within the ego's sheath.
I'll offer you sweetly with trust and grace;
So that I may know eternal solace.

The Gardener

by Mary Mc Manus

The poem, The Gardener, came to me during a meditation. For years - for decades really - I was searching. I was looking for answers to what I had lived through. I wanted to make sense out of the tragedy of my family. When I stopped looking for answers outside of myself, when I stopped grasping and when I finally listened to how my Spirit was speaking to me through a body that shut down because Spirit was cowering in a corner, the healing finally began.

This poem speaks to the importance of tending to the garden of our soul and taking time to go within. Yes, there is sorrow in life, yet the tears that fall are not in vain, but are there to water the seeds of transformation so we can grow into the fullness of our Being.

Pain is our greatest teacher if we use it to help us to awaken and blossom as the beautiful flowers our Divine Creator intended us to be. When we align with the Source of Love, weed our garden from thoughts that separate us from that Love, our hearts open and we turn our faces to the sun becoming radiant.

The Gardener

It's not about you
It's not about me
It's about something far greater
making the world a better place
What does that mean?
Who do you follow?
Do you follow your heart
distilling and discerning from teachers who went before
who now guide you?
The wisdom is in your hearts
look within and tend to the garden of your souls
using the richest soil of tenderness, kindness and compassion.
The storms of life are your best teachers
fertilizer to help you grow
water the garden with the tears of transformation
grounded in the present moment
firmly rooted in your Truth.
Pull out the weeds of jealousy, competition, discontent and self
    loathing
that choke the roots of the beautiful flowers

reach toward the light
bend with the breeze being One with all that is.

Gentle Reminder

by Krista Katrovas

I wrote this poem after contemplating the idea of regret and while meditating on a life lived with no regrets.

Gentle Reminder

If you were to die tomorrow.
or this very minute,
what would you say
what might there be left inside of you to say
before that final moment?

What if you woke tomorrow
and the person nearest and dearest to you
was not there?
What would you wish
you had spent more time doing with them?
What would you want or need to do
to make yourself feel more complete?

And if this were the last thing
you were ever to read
let me give you
all my heart,
all the songs within my mind,
every dance left inside these bones,
let me remind you of how precious you are.

Read this every morning when you rise,
post it to a mirror,
next to the coffee pot,
wherever you can see it
and repeat these last few lines
before the start of your day,
or before bed:

"I am loved, I am beautiful,
I am smart, important,
and will never forget,
to be kind to myself
to listen to my needs, desires, and wants,
even if they seem silly,
because spirit talks to me that way,
and I am a Goddess
and will treat myself as such,
every single day,
even if only for an hour, or two,
even if only for a brief moment.
I am love."

Woman As I

by Maureen Kwiat Meshenberg

I wrote this poem to embrace the both sides of my "She". I see my fallings and my risings, always bringing me back to the peace of my soul. My writing explosion of poetry has been recent, since the ending of a 20-year marriage 3 years ago. It left me broken, bruised and feeling a pain so unbearable I thought I would never get through it.

Even when I feel the pain of all that has happened to me, I see the strength that has delivered me, and bringing me to the releasing of my soul through writing.

Woman as I

Woman am I,
I see the opening-
like a slit of light,
against my black.
I touch it and,
it floods through who I am.
Woman am I,
feeling my fear,
but pressing forward-
with diligence,
through every tear,
I've come to realize-
pain becomes my delivering strength,
it moves me to compassion.
I will not belittle myself,
Woman who I am-
I see my failures turn to conquests,
as I turn to my sacred place-
in me...
my conscious understanding,
moving pass the human mirror of me-
delicately seeing my peace,
through to the opening of my soul.

Gratitude

by Ruth Calder Murphy

From time to time, I find it refreshing and uplifting to list the things for which I'm grateful. Sometimes, I do it when I go for a run – I see whether, over the course of several miles' running, I can keep the list growing and not run out of new things to add.

It's incredible, how many things there are! Even in the difficult times, even in the dark times, the list is long and sometimes startling. On this occasion, I wrote part of my list into a poem...

"For healthy days
and strong days,
for days when I can touch the stars -
days that keep me from the brink on the other days..."

Yes; there are those "other days"; it's not helpful or healthy to deny it, but I'm grateful that so far, the stars I've touched in the "strong times" are still there in the dark times - even when they're obscured and I can't see them, let alone reach them, for a while - reminding me that dawn is just over the horizon.

Gratitude

For the small things;
For smiles,
and sunbeams,
for the brightest crimson leaf
on the pavement,
for dewy cobwebs
and the sun-dappled woodland path.
For the sound of laughter
and the song of birds,
the velvet dark that cossets sleep
and the return of day to banish nightmares,
for fruit
and porridge oats,
water
and coffee,
for tea in my big, purple mug.
For healthy days
and strong days,

for days when I can touch the stars -
days that keep me from the brink on the other days...
For the warmth of love
and the cooling touch of acceptance.
For these things:
for hope,
for a future,
for the circle of life,
I am grateful.

I Strive to Grow

by Edith Lazenby

I wrote this thinking about the New Year: I had had coffee with a new friend and we were sharing about our mutual challenges and I was talking about how we are both survivors. Yet in my determination to survive I always want more than that.

I want to grow, change, learn, blossom, and thrive. And my new friend shared that, that morning she realized she too wanted to do more than survive. I think sometimes life is just so challenging all we can do is survive, but we have a moment when we know we *will* survive and we want more.

I Strive to Grow

The night chill warms my heart
With the new moon.
I have the blessing
Of much to do: clothes need folding,
Rugs need vacuuming, thank you notes
Need writing, dishwasher is running,
Kitties want loving and my hopes fly
Feathered by prayers that dream
Of love and goodness with buds

With petals softened by compassion's
Care and healing roots that reach
From the sky to earth, my heart to soul,
Fed by a light nothing can darken
As I nestle my Muse whose words pamper
What I know enabling me to do more than survive,
Supported by willingness—I strive to grow.

Hearts

by Sarah Courtney Dean

We all, as poets, have tender hearts. And this is a fact that should be celebrated! Yes our hearts can be broken so easily but through our poetry they can be made whole again.

Hearts

My heart is a thousand years old
So you think it would be wrinkled like a prune
But not so
The truth is, it is delicate
And easily broken.
I try to make it less so
Try to make it not care
In a world that give it many lessons
But it bounces back
Time
After
Time
And stays eternally
Young.

To come across a friend of the soul
is the reassurance of ten thousand loving arms
wrapping themselves around you.

Tina Tadiya Nissinen

6

Relationships

Magic is sparked between human hearts. It's where an infinite space is created in which anything can happen. Jung described the mingling of two people much like the mixing of two chemical substances: "if there's a reaction, both are transformed." Rilke, on the other hand, wrote about the distances that exist between even the closest of human beings, as indispensable to true growth. But whether in union or separation, hearts share a language in which poets are most certainly fluent.

The language of the heart saturates the following pages. Yet, as it floods the arena of our relationships with ourselves and others, it doesn't do so without traversing the bridge that connects the two. For in diving deeply into others' hearts, we inevitably awaken parts of our own beings. Like migrating butterflies shifting weather patterns on the other side of the planet, and bees pollinating flowers, human hearts are also part of a natural design that celebrates interconnections. This interdependence we all share is responsible for our very sustenance.

Intuitively aware of this phenomenon, a spiritual poet is extra sensitive to the absence or presence of nourishment in a relationship. Learning to use satiation and hunger equally as passages to divinity, she clothes her heart in pretty paradoxes. Both a nomad and a homebody, indiscriminate and exclusive, fierce and delicate, the heart of a poetess is exercised in the most amazing ways when it's engaged with the hearts of others. Whether with parents, siblings, teachers, friends, spouses, children, etc, the journeys poetic hearts take in their relationships with others never fail to reveal portions of the universal heart.

Ever since antiquity, humans have recorded the mystical quality that seems to appear when two or more hearts converge. For it's through our relationships with other living beings in this world that we feel most uplifted. As we learn to speak each other's heart languages, we seem to simultaneously acquire a *divine* language: something tangible and timeless we call love, as essential to our survival as oxygen. In synchronizing their poetic outpourings with this divine heartbeat, we hear these women—almost trancelike—enter into explorations of love's velvety and prickly textures. Or *is it* love?...some ask, still achy from the seams of a torn heart, their voices laced with longings. While others become colorful word seamstresses, unmistakably embroidering love into their verses, with threads spun from their own souls.

In this chapter, the poets carve thoughtful paths between their relationships with others, and their relationships with love. With honest strides, they explore the boundaries of caged hearts and the constraining societal views of marriage, as we feel them reaching into eternity through the immediate relationships in their lives. As they send children off to school, anticipate the birth of grandchildren, and nod off by the fire with their soul mates, we hear these sensitive souls defining love, searching for it, and celebrating it. Drawing parallels between tending to gardens and tending to our hearts, these poets remind us that while gardens can be contained, love cannot. It is this boundless quality of love that the following poems reflect.

Birthing

by Nancy Carlson

Mothering and being mothered is a life long process. Taking many forms as we all go through the phases of our lives and circumstances. A deep relationship with self and the other: our children, mother, friends and clients. I am a mother of two: a daughter and son, both young adults and on their own. My own mother passed three years ago. It's very sacred work and way of being: this mother-ness!

Recently I have felt that in my life there is another kind of birth that requires mothering. Similar to what I felt with my children. A sacred archetype of mother, as I continue to birth my Self (soul) with the grace of the Divine Mother. Death and re-birth... And now I feel very full, heavy with "child"...waiting. And my poem speaks of this experience.

Birthing

As the mother, in gestation, preparing for birthing,
nurturing, holding, loving.
Carefully choosing pure nutrients
for the one to be born.
Providing a calm, warm, soft environment,
for that which is coming
Almost ready...
I am given wisdom, ancient knowledge,
steadiness, patience and strength.
The structure to hold, in this process.
Joy, anticipation, enthusiasm,
faith in the mystery, what will be.
Grace...
Letting go of....fear, doubt, the pain of birth,
anything that does not support this new birth,
what was...
Having complete trust and faith
to embrace this child
as a new life, a new way of being.
Bringing in all that sustains, maintains and celebrates.
Courage and greatness...
Delightful, this new life and way.
Continuing to birth, again and again,
more Light, more Love.
Holding in my hands,
my center, my heart, my Self
and All others, as they are me.

Sending Them Off to School
by Ruth Calder Murphy

Motherhood has changed me. It has taught me more than any other single thing - about Creativity, about Time and about Divinity.

Creativity is important to me. It is water and air to me. If I can't create, I'm like a fish out of water and, even in the constant turnover of mothering days I need time out, to paint and to write. But, what I've also learned, is that motherhood is quintessentially creative. First, it creates a brand new life, then, it births brand new moments, perspectives, lessons. It helps us - parents and children - to see the world in new ways and to connect with the Creator, within and without. Motherhood has helped me to see all sorts of things in a new, Creative light.

Then, there's Time. The passing of time, the juggling of Time and the dawning realization that Now is all we have. Now. Because every moment is Now. Tomorrow, today will be in the past and only "Now" will remain. One day, I will be old and my children will be elsewhere and then, THAT will be "Now". This is the lesson I'm learning: To be here, now.

And there's the lesson of Divinity - of Spirit. My heartstrings are interwoven with those of my children - my babies will always be a part of me... yet, I have to let go. My love for them is unconditional; I give them their lives, even as I recognize that in doing so, I'm letting go of pieces of my own heart. At the same time, we are forever connected and in giving away, I am gaining inestimable treasure. This is love. This is Divine.

Sending Them Off to School

I have three tiny babies,
I love them dearly,
I fill their days with cuddles

and kisses and with ME;
I take them to the playground,
I traipse them round the town
and sing them lovely lullabies
as the sun goes down.
But recently, I've noticed,
they're not around so much.
suddenly there's space and time
for thoughts - and tea - and such.
I breathe the gentle silence,
enjoy Creative Space...
but there are times when I just miss
my babies, round the place.
I wouldn't mind so much, I think,
if Time had played more fair -
but no, it seems no sooner born
than they're no longer there.
I know the culprit, and approve -
I'll play it by the rule
and know that it's not terrible
to send them off to school...
But still, I see the memories,
and wonder when they passed,
turning babies into children -
and how it went SO FAST.

Close to Lisa

by Margaret Vidale

This is one of my earliest poems. I wrote it when our daughter Lisa was pregnant with our first grandson. I was so full of joy and wonder, I intuitively stretched out my heart and mind, striving to find the right words. Now I believe I was stretching towards a vast, spiritual power, which reached back to me and, indeed, reaches to all of us. I have been stretching ever since!

Close to Lisa

Seated close to me, my daughter
Lisa is lost in thought.
Small, sweet smiles
play along the curve of her delicate lips.

She rubs her round belly
with soothing, circular motion;
her message is repeated
again and again —
I am here, I love you.

Once my baby girl, now a kind
wise woman, she carries forward
Life's miraculous cycle,
just as I did so many years ago.

Life creating life,
the miracle is repeated
again and again,
each birth unique and astounding
each birth familiar and old as time.

As I watch her transformation
my heart expands with joy and gratitude,
for surely I am the luckiest of grandmothers
to be here, seated close to Lisa.

On the Other Side of the Fence

by Rosemerry Wahtola Trommer

Sometimes we see something in the outer world that is the perfect
mirror for what is happening inside of us. We were wandering

through the community gardens in Helsinki—dozens of beautifully cared for plots with little cottages on each. I could not help but admire not only the gardens, but also the determination and care that I knew had gone into them. It made me think of love.

How it seems as if it should be so simple to tend to a relationship—to nurture it and give it enough energy and time that it might flourish. But it doesn't always work that way. Does it ever work that way?

The longing to love is simple, but real life can be very messy, and despite our best intentions, we can often destroy the things we thought we were caring for. Though a garden can be contained, love cannot.

On the Other Side of the Fence

A low fence lined
with wild roses.

Two white chairs
and a round white table.

Scent of a recent
afternoon rain.

Beet greens proud,
crimson veined and tall

and the gooseberries swollen
nearly red.

In this small garden
everything tended.

In me
a longing like that.

Transform Again

by Alexandra Moga

I've observed a general hesitation in my generation towards marriage and commitment. We seem to be holding off on marriage and making families, wanting instead to experience as much independence and freedom from dreaded stagnation as possible until we commit, thinking commitment to be the end of our personal evolutions.

"Transform Again" is about keeping the spark of transformation alive on a deeper level, it's meant to inspire a dynamic relationship with the self and with others, in the direction of acceptance and flexibility, regardless of external status.

In the end, we are always transforming, and coming to that realization, we might be able to steady ourselves in that, make the most of it, and find a home in the unchanging, eternal stream of love.

Transform Again

Transform again
So I can say I thought I knew you back when
Happily whisper to my heart in a wink,
I just don't know him like I did

Transformed again
While that dress I'm in looks foreign to your constant eyes
Still settles on your soul's remembered ties
Sparks your mellow memory in a nick of causeless time

Transform again
To please that eternal form
As it watches your forgetfulness
Lose your little self to the ultimate
Die to live, die to live

Transformed again
Squirming, emerging against the tides
Bashed into false dreams countless times
Finally waking restless mind
To the lightness of an ebbing sigh

Transform again
Questions cloaked in answers
Wrangled into extra time
Compromise broken control
And let your soul sweetly abide

Transformed again
An instrument in those knowing hands
Dropped the sound of suffering
Deliver me your tonic place of rest
Appealing fallen to uncover best

Transform again
Lift the veil, receive a taste
Bridge low lands and the mirrored page
Invest in cleansing ways to see the same
If you will, reunite on the eternal train

Transformed again
Calling out your name
From an ocean of darkness, this ever-changing game
Hearing, a new plant springs to sustain
Roots to the source, an evergreen thumb digging to remain

Transformed again
By this love like a river
Feeding rapid flames in veins to steady
A nearer kind of me, simply and no longer
Transformed again

Where is Love?

by Gwen Potts

This poem was written whilst exploring the meaning of love and relationships. Especially our tendency to get lost in our partner, and the importance of remaining in our own center, as difficult as that can be at times!

Where is Love?

Is love in the passionate and magnetic pull that brings two lovers
    together?
Or in the gentle gaze into each other's eyes:
The reflection of Your soul.

Is love in the raw passion of sexual interaction:
Burning like a wild fire to the core?
Or in the energetic embrace
That can be felt without even touching.

Is love in the pain and despair of separation?
Or in the feeling of completeness
Already within the soul.

Is love in the reflection of the other?
But what is reflecting?
Other than the love we already have within.

Is love in what the other can give to us?
Or in the gifts we uncover as they hold up the mirror?

Is love to be found in energetic exchanges,
Or the feeling of being fully centered within ourselves?

Can love be found through another or by another?
Or are we the only one who holds the key to our true selves?

Love has a purpose!
This is to discover:
That we already Are the love we seek.

Heart Matters

by Carolyn Riker

When I write *sometimes* the words flow easily. Lately it's been more of a staccato. My rhythm lingers in the rests as I reflect in the silence. I've been reflecting intensely for a month now and I think I understand why.

This poem is about various relationships. Like many of our interactions it can get confusing when it appears one way and then seemingly changes into another. It is about boundaries. Where do we begin and end? *"Ultimately, of course, there is no other, and you are always meeting yourself." Eckhart Tolle*

When I settle my mind, and I let down the fences placed to protect my heart, I can see the lichen that clings. Messages can be sent and learned by everyone we meet. *"Be grateful for whoever comes, because each has been sent as a guide from beyond." Rumi*

What we do with those moments of insight can be equally heart wrenching, expansive, liberating, joyful and a bit terrifying. Yet, letting go of what holds us back is as necessary as pruning roses. New growth will come in the eclipses of our heart. Blocking the growth only delays the progress and adds another cage around the heart. This poem reflects an inner journey of exploring boundaries, old and new.

Heart Matters

Sorting through the rubble
I met a rock
Stable and real
My own world dark and crumbled
Obstacles plenty but replaced by stepping stones
And I grew
Inner resilience was ignited
Heart mattered
Gratitude
Mind learned to dance with the Moon
As a connection grew the boundaries became diffused.
Spiritual fate
The storm became rough
Waves crashed
Patterns repeat
Imploding and exploding
An ebb and flow of old mixed with new
Fear and betrayal
Eroded the core
Exposed the Ego
An avalanche of mistrust
Set off echoes of the past
The tides uncovered the source
An abandoned child emerged shaken and hurt
Where boundaries of consistency were few.
The rock was a mirror of me.
It has now returned to the sea.
A weathered worn pebble remains on the beach
I carry it in the pocket of my heart.
I reconnected a lost part of me reflected in you.

Have Wings, Will Fly

by Latika Teotia

When relationships break, one's self-esteem also goes through turmoil. It then becomes very difficult for a woman to rise again and see herself worthy of Love and Life. Yet when I look back on my own broken relationship, I feel as if it happened for my spiritual growth. I have no hard feelings about my past. In fact, I feel it taught me, and it opened me, into a flowering phase of my life. Whatever I am now, I owe, in part, to that bad relationship.

I believe by love and positive thinking, one can heal their past and embrace the present...I would conclude in a sentence that 'Acceptance is the Key Of Life'

Have Wings, Will Fly

Sometimes, things don't work out right
And you just have to say 'bye'
Every tear comes to dry
All that matters is 'belief in one's own self'
I won't let sorrow hurt me anymore
I will be stronger than before
My hope won't desert me
I am not alone anymore
I can now say this is mine
You can't take it
I 'now' believe in myself
I can...I will...fly...
I have wings
I will fly!

Only Love

by Cassandra Alls

This poem was inspired after reuniting with an old friend after 20 years. It was a beautiful reminder that no matter the time, distance, circumstance or beliefs, love is ever present.

Our minds may forget but our soul remembers the connections that never fade. We are all connected in the most powerful energy of The Universe. We are united and connected in Love.

Only Love

We've been connected all along, through many lifetimes and light years. You've found me in each one, flying through the Universe with only your soul as radar.

You don't know where you are going, but your heart does. When you reach your destination your heart, your soul, your *Spirit* explodes with the energy that remembers. There is a knowing even if the mind fights it. The *Spirit* is stronger, but you will not listen.

We live in an illusion fighting through the distractions, ignoring the messages that eat away at our being. Pay attention my Love; it's real, it never ends. Love is eternal.

In silence you found me. In the darkness I saw your eyes open and connect with mine, as if we were there again. In that place where no words exist, but the soul hears the message.

Be with me, if only in your heart and remember. Remember that there is no time, there is no place, there is only now and only *Love*.

I Love

by Maru Garcia

What does it mean to really love someone? Perhaps the best way to answer that is to look at ourselves when we are feeling loved by someone. What is that experience like? For me it's a feeling of amazement that someone loves me in spite of myself!

When I am feeling really loved, the person whom I'm feeling loved by does so in spite of all my defects, all my frailties, all my mistakes and imperfections. They love me through my darkest nights and regardless of all the emotional baggage I come with.

This kind of love leaves me in awe, for it is all embracing. It is patient. It is not intent on changing me. It is not forceful. It does not withdraw when I don't meet its conditions, because it has none. It is something I can rely on no matter what.

Real love knows that I am a package deal: with pretty parts and ugly ones too. It receives me as I am at any given moment in time, even when I'm a handful, even when I'm upset, even when I'm lost. And it does so without ever waning. In fact, it does just the opposite. This love grows! It is not stagnant. It blossoms in the most dynamic, energizing ways.

True love is forgiving and knows that I, myself, am not perfect at loving, yet loves me anyway. This kind of love is reciprocal and flows in two directions just as enthusiastically. It is not unrequited love. And it does not leave to find something higher, or better. For true love has faith that the purest love can be cultivated even between human hearts, as we are all divine at our cores.

I believe that we each may have different conceptions of what love is. So many cultures and traditions around the world and across times have attempted to define love, to encapsulate love's boundlessness within the limits of words. Some speak of different kinds of love, and degrees of loving. Some love is more pure than others.

I believe we all long to be loved, and are trying our best to love others.

It is our nature. It is at the core of why we exist. As I see it, the closer we are to loving purely, the closer we are to being ourselves and fulfilling out life's purpose.

So, as far as perfect lovers go: I think we are all "works-in-progress". And on our way there, this poem reminds me that it's good to remember that: "Unless love includes radical acceptance, it should be called something else." Something worth meditating on today, as I take inventory of what's in my own heart.

I Love

I love what I see and what you veil
What you show or insinuate
Who you are or I choose to imagine that you are

I love you in what you lack and in what you are more than enough
I love what you share of you and what you hide
Your questions and replies
Your doubts, your certainties and masks

I love you in your simplicity and confusion
In what you shout and what you screen

I love what you ask for and what you give away
Your memories and obliviousness
Your laughter and your discontent

I love your scents, your taste and breath
What you love and what you escape.

I love you in this spot and in the distance
I love you for the love of it

Without a catch, without a map
If I were able to not love you I would still do it

I love you with the pride of loving you
I love you because I was born to

I love you in your insanity and your stillness
I love you in your joys and your despair
In your heaven and your hells
I love you how you are, exact
I just love you, intact.

The Bride

by Aparna Khanolkar

L ove is the greatest longing of every human heart. I wrote this poem for a deeper experience of the bride on her wedding day. Amidst all the excitement, fervor and joy is the secret of love. Yes, this is what we all long for most.

The Bride

A longing, an ache in my restless heart
Love churns, spins like a whirling dervish in divine ecstasy
Sublime sorrow, the heart yearns for a glimpse of innocence

The candles flicker in the evening breeze
Rose petals wait eagerly lest they wither if they give up hope
The curls of incense smoke play with themselves
I sit here adorned with my jewels,
sandalwood and henna on my hands,
heart open, ready
body and spirit anticipating --
your arrival, your acceptance, your love

A culmination, an end to an eternal quest
Lift the veil on my intellect
submerge me in love
Whisper in my ears of divine love, its ecstasy

This red and gold saree will not matter
as will not the gold or the tinkle of my ankle bells
My eyes are hungry, thirsty, eager to devour you in one soul gaze

Struggles, obstacles - a mere dance as I make my way to you
The one that sees me - royal, regal, with exquisite beauty and grace
This body, this mind will die one day
This heart beats its beat to the cosmic rhythm of love
It reverberates with every sound of the universe - each whisper, each
    song, each word is love from you.

The Feeling of You
by Tina Tadiya Nissinen

I cherish my friends - they are everything to me. They also get me through pretty much everything, good and bad, in life. Friends are important no matter where we are in life but in the spiritual path especially, I think, it's vital to have friends to share it with, to be a part of a community for many reasons.

In *bhakti* yoga, this is emphasized: *sanga*, meaning the company and community of others on the path, is considered to be something that we absolutely need in order to grow in and sustain our faith. Bhakti yogis are instructed to develop intimate and confidential friendships with others on the path. Loving God includes loving all of those who are dear to him.

I wrote this poem originally intending to write about how my Guru —my guide and teacher in *bhakti* yoga— feels like a friend of the soul to me, and how the very feeling of him seems to sustain my soul. But in the process of writing, I changed it from a singular friend to plural, as in "friends of the soul", realizing that God's grace comes to me - yes, in the form of my guru - but also in other friendships that nourish my soul. Besides relationships, God's grace and good will toward me sometimes takes other forms. For example, I consider the feeling of hope and faith as such good friends of my soul.

Srila Sridhara Maharaja, a beloved teacher of *bhakti*, has often been quoted saying "the environment is friendly" meaning that when we are able to see the world through the eyes of faith and love - and approach it as servants rather than exploiters - we will see how everything in our lives is indeed friendly and helping us. "A bad worker quarrels with his tools", as Sridhara Maharaja puts it. Meaning: we must start where we are and work with what we have.

What I have, personally, is a lot of sadness and sorrow, and doubt as well, to work with. And I certainly have wasted a lot of time quarreling with myself, and my circumstances. And, at times, to my regret that has created distance between me, and my friends. But what has pulled me through - and near - has always been the love of my friends, their love for my soul. This poem is dedicated to all my friends - especially to my Guru, a dearmost friend of my soul.

The Feeling of You

Dear friend of the soul,

I've been holding my distance
from you

knee-deep in
disbelief,
I have stood my ground on nothing

for fear gave me
such impossible marching orders that

my feet, for a year, refused to go
near you.

Only distance grew big in me
as I leaned into it

I became small,

holding onto
nothing

poured
of the concrete of despair

and sorrow
let me tell you -
should never feel like your only friend

but sometimes
she does

So, I stood still
wearing the heavy shoes of hesitation;
feet in the cement of my
own pouring

and the place I once hurried to,
became just a blurred vision on the horizon,

as I let the
the feeling of you
fade away;
and doubt to wear myself thin

somehow, I lost touch
of the Meaningful

let my hope
be reduced to a tiny whisper in the corners of the self

made my home into the alone and
housed myself in the smallest possible corner
of the self: shame.

I fell so far and away
from you

But then, as
the very ground beneath my stumbling
rose up to hold me

I found out that

a little hope
goes a long way

for everything holds a possibility
for entering the Meaningful.

There are two ways to live:
as though everything has meaning
or nothing

The nothing, got me nowhere

but the everything,
got me cornered: I had to face myself in all directions

pull away far enough
and you are pulled near – almost by accident.

Such is the crookedness of grace. It gets you
while you're getting away from it.

And *the something missing*
in everything

reveals
your heart's
longing for

the Meaningful

who
comes
in search of us

until you recognize her
as the very Friend you've missed all your life

and then you will see how
God has sent so many good friends to meet you on the way!

Friends of the soul, who come
with hopeful news about *the meaning of it all*

who hold your heart
in such a way that
the very feeling of them

is enough of an answer.

Dearmost friends,
coming with arms full
of
love letters to your soul

Think about it: you can be
best friends
with the Forever.

Oh my friends,

I fold the feeling of you into a corner of my heart
and keep it there, in the chambers of my
unsteady heart

ready to be pulled out when and if need be

I hold on to this, the faith of you
that gives the Meaningful into my empty arms

giving me
so much to hold onto
that I am held

from here to hope, to love
and my soul is received in such a way

that nothing can no longer
claim to fill me.

My friends,
everything about you pulls me nearer to the Meaningful

as I lean towards this feeling of you; this vastness
that's holding my heart

- and the things
it has to say to me,

my head can hardly believe it

so like an unsent letter, I hide it away, tuck it under my heart
and wonder if there's a way to say it?
Or if I can even feel it tomorrow

Still, the feeling of you

is now a space that's widening
inside of me,

and I
come out bigger
for having been in it.

Something in you,
makes my soul
come out and be near.

In the presence of friends
who love my self like their own self

distance is no longer an option.
I know this now:

to have this kind of intimacy, even for a moment,
between you and the one that needs no introducing

and to feel the vastness of that love

that somehow squeezes itself
inside your little heart and makes it bigger,

is the miracle we were born into.

The embrace is such
that your prayers become short: just wishes
for everyone to have friends like this!

To come across a friend of the soul
is the reassurance of ten thousand loving arms
wrapping themselves around you

To know that God has such friends for your soul
makes everything appear friendly;

you might even begin to befriend
the stranger in your own self,

so difficult to love, to embrace

for it's like spring, when someone receives you
like this:
you grow without trying to.

And friends like this
who welcome your soul,
like the sun welcomes the day

by
giving it
it's light: illuminates

both
your absolute need for mercy
and the existence of it –

God does not just give grace
- she becomes it

and you see it
in your friend's smiling face – in your own smile, too

like a thousand suns
appearing across the horizon of your heart

and you feel it,
as the heart you've held closed
now pours itself out
almost involuntarily

What the world needs
is this space
widening in every heart

So,
may *the something missing*
lead you there

and your soul come to know
the embrace of such Friends

may the feeling of them
guide you

to the Meaningful
in search of you.

Look around: Everything wants to be your friend.

Yet Love Remains

by Ginny Brannan

Sometimes we come across something that speaks to us as though it were our own. This happened for me when I read "When You Are Old" by William Butler Yeats. It reminded me of the life I've shared with my husband of almost 32 years. In that time we have certainly weathered many storms; yet we survive, our bond even stronger.

I decided to use the words of Yeats to weave a Glosa, a very old form of poetry that begins with a quote of four lines from a well-known poet, in this case Yeats, and expands the theme into four ten-line stanzas, the lines of the poet used to conclude each stanza. Since this form is often used to pay tribute, I pay tribute to my best friend, my soulmate, my husband; and the life we share together.

163

Yet Love Remains

"When you are old and grey and full of sleep,
And nodding by the fire, take down this book,
And slowly read, and dream of the soft look
Your eyes had once, and of their shadows deep..."
William Butler Yeats

I think about the sweet days of our youth,
the world was spread before us for the taking--
invincible, we weathered many storms
safety found inside each other's arms.
Discovered life together, you and I...
rappelling over cliffs and chasms deep;
wary of the monsters in the darkness--
learning that my strength resides in you.
Will love remain inside where memories steep,
when you are old and gray and full of sleep?

So many years between have come and gone
the passion found in youth not often held;
yet on occasion universe aligns,
amazing how a kindred spirit bonds
once it finds the niche where it belongs.
We couldn't know this when we undertook
to forge a life together, you and I.
Yet over time, my love for you remains.
I hear you breathing softly while I look,
and nodding by the fire, take down this book.

The one that holds the stories that we've shared
well-chronicled and inked to stay in our memory;
each page presents an instant frozen in time,
designed to be reviewed in quiet moments...
a lifetime kept in images we've saved.
I scan the scraps and photos that we took,
and settle once again on my favorite image--

given to me after we first met.
On cushions soft, I settle in this nook,
and slowly read and dream of the soft look...

in a contemplative moment it was captured--
in graying sky your eyes shown cobalt blue;
from that moment, I was captured too.
And so we came to know each other well;
to compliment the other; to complete.
I turn the page, and now it seems that sleep
beckons me to close and come to bed.
I stretch out in the hollow of your arm
to slip away and dream of white-hot heat
your eyes had once, and of their shadows deep.

This is a call for women
To know and believe
in the holiness of their bodies
The sacredness in their dance
And the power of their voice.

Zola Dubnikova

7

Sisterhood

They say that the most ancient tribes saw women as holding the same creative magic in their wombs that created the cosmos. We were known to have hearts that loved with superhuman strength and beat with the essence of life itself. Women were seen as the healers, and the teachers, and as oceans of intuitive wisdom so deep, we became known as conduits to divinity. And our powers *grew* every time we gathered as one—as sisters—before blazing fires and under full moons, leaving past peoples so awed and mystified by the bond between us, they were inevitably moved to bow before the Goddess and her many forms. Where women were nourished and adored, communities would thrive. And it was evident that there was a special *kind* of nourishment that women only drew from the company of other women.

Loving bonds between women are made of an emotional richness and complexity that has transcendent potency. Our female friends lift us. They connect us with the macrocosm when we feel overcome and overwhelmed by stressors in our microcosm. They rescue us with broader views when ours have become myopic. They flood our bodies with the soothing effects of oxytocin, unlike anything else but our own newborns, so the intimacy between us women is deep and calming, and stitched together with a most precious kind of love. It's a kind of love that nature says we can't live without. For, women are biologically designed to seek out the company of other women when we feel overcome by life. We do not respond with "fight or flight", instead, deep within us, something primal says: "unite". We seek out soul sisters because they lighten our burdens, they share in our chores, they appear like boats on the rivers of our lives when we've exhausted ourselves swimming.

There is no solace like the arms of a soul sister. She receives our heartache with gentle attendance and wraps it up in the soft shawl of her understanding. Over cups of tea and late into the night, our sister knows the harmonies to our heart's songs and sings them back to us without judgment. She is there when we stumble and accepts us the way we. She holds up mirrors to us when we've lost sight of ourselves, and blows wind into our sails when we're stagnating. Keepers of our secrets and decorators of our dreams, our sisters become the sanctuaries of our souls and the menders of our hearts. In the love women exchange with one another, we awaken a deep, spiritual oneness that speaks to the sacred. We awaken joy, inspiration, power and realization in each other. We awaken the individual goddesses we each are, and the divine Goddess we all belong to together.

This chapter celebrates the sacred bonds between women. It swells with the encouragement and appreciation we offer one another, and is perfumed with irreplaceable trust. In it, the poets speak about their soul-sisters as angels of mercy, love-vessels and sweet candies, as they take each other by the hands on morning walks and philosophize under open skies. Embracing one another's free spirits, the poets become gypsies moving to the beat of primordial tambourines, their long hair blowing the in breeze of their affections for one another. In poetry that sounds like prayers and graceful oblations, these women invite us into the temple of their hearts, where we find their sisters, seated on altars like beautiful goddesses.

Every Woman
by Nirvani Teasely

Poetry is a reflection of a poet's heart. This poem was written at a time when I was feeling such raw emotion regarding all of the beautiful and divine women in this world and their great struggles in life.

Many women are unaware of the amazing souls they are and have been beaten down by such struggles. They have come to believe they have nothing worthwhile to offer and are worthless. So often I wish I could wrap my arms around every woman who feels worthless and take all of that self-doubt and loathing and replace it with self-love.

My heart aches for the women of this world. We should see ourselves in every woman. She is my grandmother, my mother, my sister, my daughter, my friend...she is me and I am her.

Every Woman

Sometimes, I want to love every woman.
Take all my joy and hand-sew it to her heart.
Use the strongest thread, secure it as tight as I can,
Where no one, not even she, can tear it apart.

Sometimes, I want to love every woman,
Whisper profound words of adulation in her ear,
Until she believes she is her greatest fan.
And in the dark of night, my love for her will see her clear.

Sometimes, I want to love every woman,
Take her self-defeating ways, crush them under my heel,
And never again will she believe she is less than.
She'll be every girl's superhero, the Wo-Man of Steel.

Sometimes, I want to love every woman,
Maybe because I am every woman and she is me.
And no matter where she is in life, she can always start again,
For self-love is the very reflection of her, it is her heart's key.

Sisterhood

by Carolyn Riker

As each year passes, we add new friends to our circle of sisterhood. We walk with each other through our journeys. We share laughter and joy as well as tears and hardships. A foundation is built to withstand the storms.

Our friendships are a bond of steadfast trust and honesty. There's an unspoken, nonjudgmental safety net of encouragement and caring support. The candor and genuine love glows from within. We can be vulnerable and therefore brave. This is sacred to me. I wrote this poem to honor the sisterhood of friendships that have graced my life.

Sisterhood

A sacred circle of
Women joyfully gather to
Exchange and transcend
Share and respect
Centuries of divine feminine wisdom
Imparted
A synergy formed
The gift of trust
Created and cherished
Linked with fluid steps
Sustained in an exquisite vessel
The love is felt and exchanged
A tenacious tapestry
Infinite
Resilient
Courageous
Our hearts tenderly held
in sisterhood of love.

Stronger Together
by Mariann Martland

There are times in life when you feel that there is nobody who understands your pain. There is nobody to whom you can reach out or speak your lonely words. You feel completely alone, unspeakably lonely. And then, you suddenly feel held, you are alone but you no longer feel lonely in your ache.

For some this might be found in a faith, a universal connection: a sense of unity with humanity. Or this unseen force is found for many through a virtual world of words and sentiment, of shared expression, knowing and understanding.

During times of intense struggle, there have been moments when I have found connection in the most unexpected places. There have been moments when people whom I have never met have carried me through into the next moment, that had felt impossible to reach, through their writing, their words, their understanding, their shared experience.

Through these virtual, yet very real, worlds, communities can be formed where acceptance, strength and connection can be found.

Stronger Together

You sit alone.
There is no sound to hear, no voice at all.
You look for another to comfort, to care.
Nobody steps into your lonely vision.

But wait, there, in the distance
There are others moving towards you,
Stretching out their hands,
Opening their arms to hold you.

There is a community of souls who understand,
A world where people stand alongside you.
You cannot see them, you cannot hear,
But oh how you feel their warmth.

You are surrounded by love,
By acceptance; a force-field of support.
You are strong on your own.
You are stronger together.

Luz Maria

by Salyna Garcie

As we move through our daily lives we are sometimes given a glimpse into the divine in the most unlikely places. If we are paying attention, every person we meet is a holy encounter with the Beloved. Humble angels come to us clothed as ordinary people with extraordinary blessings.

This poem is inspired by one such encounter, and the deep sense of gratitude that results from experiencing grace.

Luz Maria

In this isolated never-land
Pinned between mountain peak
And river-bend
A humble angel of mercy
Walks quietly into these woods
Without need of gleaming armor
Or celestial horn
Sacred vestments of soft cotton
And comfortable shoes
Wings unfurled to a warm embrace
She is the light of compassion
Illuminating dark secrets,
Hidden maps and swallowed keys
She is the hand of kindness
Holding the broken heart in her palm
Wiping the tear from crying eye
Each meeting a holy encounter
Even as the last sand grain
Drops to the bottom
Of the two-hour glass
The love flows on
The love always flows on

No Hurry to Find Out

by Rosemerry Wahtola Trommer

I t is so wonderful to have a close friend you can talk about everything with. I am lucky to have several friends like this. One of them, Joan May, has been my Monday walking partner for several years, and on our Monday walks we talk about mundane things, what to feed our children, but also the biggest questions, such as "Who am I really?" and "What is happiness?"

With Joan, there's never a sense that we need to actually answer the question. Our discussions often dissolve into a sense of wonder and openness, even delight in not knowing. I wrote this poem after one such Monday excursion up toward Briday Veil Falls outside of Telluride.

No Hurry To Find Out

Joan asks me what happens after we die,
and I don't know, but I do know
how to stand beside the river
and see a shrine in every rock I find,

which is how I spent the day yesterday.
And I know that walking today
in the snow, every step felt like
a prayer, which is to say

I feel so very lucky to be alive,
even though I don't know who
the prayer is to—nor what the point
of praying is—except that on days like today

I overspill with gratitude
and it feels so good to say thank you
for this life that happens before we know
what happens after we die.

Your Words

by Vrinda Aguilera

Writers are people who are mediums for all of the arts. I believe this to be true because, in the right hands, the written word can be arranged to transmit emotions, experiences, sights, sounds, and tastes, calling forth and broadcasting a plethora of multifaceted sensorial experiences. All of the senses can be appealed and communicated to, albeit through the subtle channels of the written word.

Artfully painted words, colorfully chosen and carefully placed, capture the scenic beauty of a misty, dew drop covered morning meadow. A steady hand dips, dabs and wields the brush- a painter's finished masterpiece magically appears on the canvas of the reader's mind's eye.

Finely tuned words, composed and orchestrated by the poet conductor, resonate and harmonize in the mind's ear of an attentive reader. Presto! A grand symphony, fully conducted and carried out with nary an instrument to be seen. Can you hear the low notes of the wind instruments, blowing a haunting melody, accentuated by the staccato thunderclap of the percussion?

Who hasn't journeyed down a path to love's gate and opened up wide their hearts to enter into a novel of grand romantic proportions? Me? Ah, yes, I have loved and lost and loved again, many times over in the deep valleys and dizzying mountain peak settings of seductively woven intricate tales of love and intrigue.

One day as I was contemplating how I experience the writing of a dear friend as being engaging and tangible I was moved to explore and engage the gustatory sense of taste through poetry. Besides being a skilled writer and poet this friend is one of those people whose creativity isn't limited to one particular medium. She is also a gifted painter, photographer, and cook, among other things: A mistress of the arts, if you will!

My very special friend, Krishna Kanta, inspired this poem. She is the gatekeeper who generously and hospitably opens the gate for many a weary and often somewhat travel worn souls who often shyly tarry nearby, casting wistful glances her way. She'll warmly invite you in, offer you a seat, and soothe you with her kindness before lovingly offering you a moment in the sunlight. Sometimes she may have to give a little fortifying push, smiling at you with full assurance all the while.

She's an advocate for women from many different backgrounds of countries, cultures and faiths, a dedicated force whose mission is to unify and serve other women in their sojourns traversing along the path of developing authenticity in our love for ourselves, each other and, ultimately, the Supreme.

Your Words

My friend!
Your words are like
A bag of candies

I delight in their receipt.
Slowly, with anticipation,
I unwrap your writing,
Fingering the fine and delicate wrappers.
The slight, friendly rustlings
Pique my curiosity,
What's inside?

Tropical pineapple and orange sunburst Surprise
Anger, a spicy red hot cinnamon snap
Bubbling, bursting-blueberry is Joy
Pain, a cloyingly sweet, black licorice
Love is sweet and warm apple pie
Acrid and sour lemon yellow-tinged is Fear

My taste buds and heart
Relish and swoon in turn
A multitude of moods and flavors

Intertwine and linger
I sample and savor

My friend!
Your words are like
A bag of candies.

I See You

by Savitri

I remember a rainy summer day at a World Peace ceremony community event at Kew Beach garden in Toronto, where folks from all walks life collectively offered prayers for peace to every corner of the world.

I was sitting with two friends who were visiting from Indonesia when a simple but powerful gaze of someone's eyes reminded me of our eternal, spiritual abode. With heart opened, senses heightened, spirit and nature danced together wildly within and this poem was born.

I See You

in the wise counsel of the elders
in the innocence of little children and street wisdom of the youth
in the sweet embrace and playful exchange of dear friends
in the warm sunshine touching my skin
in the soft Summer breeze playing with my long hair
in every step of Life's ecstatic dance
in each gamelan tune and echo of the gongs
in the dewy grass and crisp white sand I danced on this morning
in the wispy wild flowers swaying gracefully
in the glitters of the stars and the soft light of the moon
in the early morning sun and late night silence
in the sacred sound vibrating in my veins, rejoicing in my heart

in the depth of soul-reaching gaze of someone's eyes that reminds
  me of home

Through melting heart and tears of gratitude,
I see You,
Beloved

Lady Wisdom

by Kiernan Antares

Sophia...Sophia... I contemplate courage as I feel that it's not courage we seek to deal with what life brings us, but rather, courage to *look within*: to see what we are holding on to, our own follies and dysfunctions, and the courage to release them!

For it is in the release that we open ourselves to the unknown world/ life that lays beyond and that is what we fear. Poetry and painting are my spiritual practices: ways in which I explore my inner worlds and become who I wish to be in the world.

Lady Wisdom

Ah... the shimmering light
illuminates
the Me within me
the You within you
the World within the world.

The translucent rainbow colorsdance,
weaving in and around,
dipping and swirling,
down and down and down
and up and up and up.

Beckoning the wild woman
naked and free.

Oh yes... She emerges
giving birth to herself anew
from the deep dark abyss
to the light of day.

Come!
Sing and dance
and moan in ecstasy
with me.

Throw back your head
and let loose
wildly

Into Infinite Bliss...
The Land of Lady Wisdom.

A Blessing for Life
by Solodad Maria

Times are merging. I have noticed through my work with tribal and indigenous peoples that the healing methods of the past are being resurrected today, in our present times.

I offer you this blessing in the spirit of ancient times, when women gathered together —as we are doing here- to elevate one another. Such heartfelt openness blesses our lives from within. The woman who sees beyond illusion is freeing herself and others.

Namaste, my sisters of heart and soul!

A Blessing for Life

Blessed one, deep inside
I open to thee and embrace your being
Sacred woman, sacred soul, we are blessed
To know each other and all that is ...

From the blessed one who created all
I fuse with thee and open my heart
To the longing and depth of all
That we know...together...
Forever blessed with life.

In knowing this...I awaken my soul
To the holy hour of sacred one
Who resides so deep and is known as "I"
I welcome you here to be blessed inside.

My woman of soul, you are blessed...
With life!
I know you are with me, amidst the deep
Longing to free you...as you are "I"
I accept your wisdom and soul as myself.

In longing for life, the woman inside
Sweetens the gifts, that her pure heart knows
Are seated within the blessings of the "One"
My heart is at peace, knowing...
You are free!

Blessed woman, all that you are...
I love your magic! Your Divine soul!
I am awakened to you...knowing you
As "I"...I reside with you...
Everlasting soul...

Gypsy Woman

by Jacqui Lalita

There is a gypsy inside of every woman. I have devoted my life to helping women release that free spirit within them that dances in the moonlight. May this poem help you find and awaken the Gypsy Woman in you, and set her free with a spirit of magic and grace, into your life!

Gypsy Woman

Gypsy Woman sleeps outdoors
to be close to the wild call of coyote and crow
who remind her to always hold hands with freedom.
By night pure molecules of air laden with stardust
blanket her dreams
She spins tin cans of trust into golden opportunity
light and dark into effervescent rainbows of inspiration,
Passion and purpose adorn each adventure
to beckon her imagination.

She is a wisdom seeker in flowing skirt
and a pocket full of intuition
that carries her across landscapes and cultures,
down rivers and up mountains,
with tambourine on one hip and trust on another.

She is a close friend of plant kin, an ally of ancient ways
dancing naked under full moons
whole and holy across the days.
She makes love at any hour
and brews her magic in the night
and with bare feet she goes
spinningearthly breath into rays of light!

Gypsy woman! Gypsy woman!
Powerful is your stance!
Riding the tails of comets with a body made to dance!

Gypsy woman! Gypsy woman!
Glorious are your wings!
Riding the crest of waves with a soul that forever sings!

You twirl your dress as you spin
and the Gods come closer to peek
Oh Gypsy Woman, you are the freedom
each soul silently seeks.

Lover of life, wandering wayfarer,
fragrant gypsy moving to the beat of tambourines,
at home you are in the forest, dreaming in the desert,
visioning by the sea, wild hair flowing on the breeze,
your heart is ever-free!
Moving from village to village
naked as the moon,
skin glistening in the sun,
some raise their eyebrows as you pass
Beautiful woman come undone!

Your caravan is the Beloved,
your tribe spreads far and wide,
there is magic where you are
down double rainbows how you slide!
Go now to the shores of Avalon
or the mountain's mystic heights
loving every fearless moment, night by starry night!

Shake My Shakti Free

by Krishna Kanta Dasi

In the most ancient cultures, all around the world, everything revolved around adoring the Goddess. Once upon a time, the universe was seen as the Goddesses womb and all of us her creative energies. In India, one of her many names is Shakti, the primordial force woven into the cosmos, the Sacred Mother nourishing all life and empowering us from within.

According to the Yoga tradition of India, at our core we are all made of Shakti: divine feminine consciousness. It is believed that our life is meant to awaken this dormant goddess within, and engage her in the creative service of the Supreme Goddess, known as Radha in Sanskrit.

From the Bhakti Yoga perspective we are all Radha's servants, assisting her in fueling the love she exchanges with Krishna, her Divine Beloved. Yoga in Sanskrit means "to link", or "connect". It is this Divine Love that yoga is meant to connect us with, and this Love is capable of expressing itself through each of us, tiny goddesses, if only we let it.

When I doubt myself, or feel insecurities or fears swelling within me, I know I've disconnected from my inner goddess: My shakti is stuck and my love is not flowing so freely. That's when I become restless and achy to set her free again so she can dance!

Shake My Shakti Free

I know you from the heartbeat
Within my mother's womb,
Soothing like a mantra
That transports beyond the tomb.

I know you in the silhouette
Of mountains as you rest,
Sweet nectar inside of flowers
Warm milk from mother's breast.

Oh! Goddess! You illuminate
The divine essence at my core,
Inviting me to exhale light
Through every single pore.

Oh! Goddess! I think I feel you
Conspiring with my heart
To move me into blossoming
My petals opening apart.

I long to shake my shakti free
Let my soul run bare
Dance like no one's looking
Let down my untamed hair.

I long to let my wildness out
Splash like ocean waves
Swell like tides that draw
Precious treasures from their caves.

So jingle me like an ankle bell
that adorns your dancing feet,
Swirl my life with your beauty
in sweet, syncopated beats.

Brew me in your magic cauldron
Like a potion that will enchant
Strike from my vocabulary
The useless phrase "I can't".

Oh! Goddess! I can feel you now
Flowing through my veins
You animate the love-dances
In me I can't contain.

You inspire my inner journey
The unfurling of my heart,
As doubts and fears abandon me

And insecurities depart,
Marking the celebration
Of my life's new start.

Shiva's Wild Woman

by Nirvani Teasley

Every woman is a Goddess! She has great Divine potential and need only tap into it to find the creative spirit of *shakti* that runs through her veins. She is all that is wild and free, yet full of beauty and grace. She is a paradox in every sense of the word. This poem is a metaphor for the Divine Feminine present in every woman.

Shiva's Wild Woman

I am femininity embodied,
Deity made flesh, perfection
Embedded in flaw.
Un-submissive feminist,
Freedom-fighting,
Barefoot mama on a mission
To strengthen the sisterhood of souls.
The androgynous love, pouring
From my cosmic yoni
Paints the world in supernatural perceptions.
To one I am femme fatale,
Dangerously sacrilegious, ego-stripping
Mata Hari-esque.
To another, the primordial paradox,
The unsolvable puzzle.
To my Self, the constant
Creator and destroyer
Dancing my way

Through the universe.
Some call me
Shiva's wild woman.

Wild Woman Creation Story
by Jacqui Lalita

This poem was written in a blaze of creation. It emerged during a silent hike through the majestic redwood forest of Northern California. It celebrates the divine feminine mystery alive inside all things.

Wild Woman Creation Story

In a time outside of time, before the dawn of Adam and Eve
the spirit of Wild Woman was immaculately conceived...
Galactic gyrations and spirals of light gave Wild Woman
the gift of flight

She came as crashing thunder, pouring down the rain
and the Universe from this moment
would never be the same

Wild Woman parted her lips to sing and gave the birds their destined
    wings
Wild Woman shook her hips to dance and colored the world in a state
    of trance

The winds began to roll, the wolves began to howl and there upon her
    shoulder sat all-seeing totem owl

From bursting girth she gave birth to Earth
From her third eye came the sky
Such joy that the birds had found their home
inspired her to cry

She stirred her tears into a passionate potion that soon became
    wide open ocean
With outstretched arms she began to whirl and the spirit of dolphins
    came unfurled

Wild woman spread her legs laying embryos and crystal eggs
stones and bones, gushing rivers, vital livers
She shivered all the world alive amidst orgasmic quivers

The spirit of Shiva and Shakti simultaneously revealed
lush gardens exploding with fruits waiting to be unpeeled...

Wild Woman dreamed a mighty lion to guide the way to the land of Zion
She planted fields of corn and rice seeding ripe paradise

She was maiden, mother and wise old crone
who contained all mysteries to the great unknown
She came like thunder before the dawn of time
delivering the holy word in spellbound lyric rhyme

In a flash of light
Wild Woman appeared to set this Universe free
then she hid herself in the deepest depths
inside you and me.

Ode To The Woman Within

by Helene Averous

I believe we learn how to best honor the women in the world when we first allow the flow of our hearts to honor the woman within: the woman we are. We have a great debt to this woman.

This feeling of gratitude to the woman in me —the one present and caring—overwhelmed me and released this poem from my heart. For to the woman within, I bow. I am born as a daughter, a sister, a wife, a mother, but before all, a human being with a heart in a woman's body, which I honor.

Ode to the Woman Within

To the woman who carries water to quench my thirst, I bow
To the woman who gave me life, I bow
To the woman who wipes my tears, I bow
To the woman who keeps on feeding my heart, I bow
To the woman who is tender with me, I bow
To the woman who cries, I bow
To the woman who prays, I bow
To the woman who is grateful, I bow
To the woman who suffers, I bow
To the woman who keeps on loving, I bow
To the woman who nurtures my soul, I bow
To the sacred woman, I bow

~ Om

In the Absence of Sisterhood
by Del-Rita Butler

I don't know where I would be without the love and support of my sisters. These women have been there for me when I am laughing and they have cradled me during those cries that make your body shudder and heave with sadness. They've helped me put my life in perspective over and over again. Reminding me that we've been in that dark place before and we might be there again.... but we made it through.

These women have carried me and I have carried them. They have kept my deepest secrets and stayed humble in the process. They have accompanied me on my Spiritual Journeys and encouraged me to recite my Intentions under the glow of a Full Moon. In another time and place we have dance naked and sang the songs whispered by Earth Mother. I know these women and I have walked, run and crawled with them. They are my soul-mates and the loves of my life.

The other day I was wondering what my life would be without them. What I realized is their absence would be so great that would look for them. I would know that something was missing and I would constantly look over my shoulder and into the faces of strangers. I know this to be true because I looked around every corner until each one of them came into my life to complete me.

In the Absence of Sisterhood

I took a walk today to find my shadow
The first place I looked was near the ocean
I followed the scent of the salt-sprayed air
I sniffed the mussels abandoned by the tide
    and I looked for you
I called your spirit and waited for you to respond
You did not answer my cries and I could not find you

I went for a run today throughout the park
I ran beneath the Willow tree with the wispy branches
    over the bridge near the stream filled with geese
I jumped over the low fence we called a hurdle
    while I counted my breaths
I allowed the air to fill my lungs and energize me
But I did not see you there and you did not answer

I went to the market today on the hilly side of town
I thumped the melons and squeezed the peaches
I marveled at all the vibrant colors of the fruits
    when they are permitted to ripen on the vine
        the way nature intended
I purchased soap scented with lavender in which to bathe,
I really needed to relax and I sorely feel your absence

You were my shadow during each new lesson,
    staying close and quiet
mimicking my moves in observation and respect,

hiding when I needed the right amount of space
      to make an absolute wrong decision!
I laughed with you until my face hurt and I had cramps
      beneath my ribs,
I wear this memory of bonding love
      and intrinsic peace like a shawl
Our sisterhood is strength and compassion
      of knowing without words and silent sighs
We have travelled centuries in pairs and threes
wearing costumes of lace, polyester and denim
you saved me from the singular........ time and time again

I cannot live my life without my sister-love
the want of a sister should be heralded as a need
when we meet again,
      we will pick up from that last conversation
      and you will have the last word
            and I will listen mindfully

Return to The Temple

by Zola Dubnikova

Where women thrive communities thrive. After seeing the ways in which women can be disenfranchised from their personal power and divinity in so many ways in many parts of the world, I devoted myself to using healing forms of dance to uplift women, heal their wounds, and reconnect them to their divine source.

I pray to empower women in body, heart, voice and spirit to become vessels of divine powerful expression. This is my prayer for all women: for myself, for my daughter, and for you.

Return to The Temple

This dance is a prayer
A prayer for The Earth and therefore
A prayer for women.

This is a call for women
To know and believe
in the holiness of their bodies
The sacredness in their dance
And the power of their voice.

A prayer for all women
who do not express themselves
Who hold themselves back
Who do not know
their own power
As creators
As healers,
As givers of life.

My prayer is a prayer for women
Women who are not allowed
to dance and sing
Or express themselves
in any way.

A prayer for men who do not believe
Women should dance in public.

My dance is the voice of women
who are trapped
In a life where they have no voice.

My prayer is for the young girls
who get sold into marriage
At eight years old to old men

And who die at the hands of cultures
Who permit such atrocities
to continue and continue.

My prayer is for young girls
Who are sold into sex slavery
and contract illnesses
they didn't even know existed.
My prayer is for these girls
who never have the chance to be girls.

My prayer is for the men
Whose unpunished violence and terror
against women and against The Earth
is permitted in this world.

My prayer is a dance for The Earth
My prayer is a dance for women
My prayer is a calling
for the women to return to the temple.

Listen to your soul-song
And allow your soul to resonate
With the shiver of the strings
plucked by the Source
of the music of the stars.

Linda Yael Schiller

8

Divinity

Our human experience will undoubtedly include moments in which we are struck by beauty, awed by wisdom, or moved by emotion in such a way that we have transcended our former understanding of reality. This new vista is so deeply satisfying that it can only be described as a wondrous peek into Divinity: one that leaves us with an insatiable longing for more. For we feel *more alive* when we are connected to the Divine, more complete. And though our individual relationships with the Divine are as unique as we are, we human beings—in our eagerness to communicate the greatness of such an experience to others— have attempted to map out paths to the Divine.

Across traditions, it is the trails blazed by poets that have given us the closest sense of what it's like to mingle with the sacred. The poets of antiquity often describe the soul, as a beautiful, winged creature, most often appearing as a butterfly in the garden of spiritual life. These beautiful insects became powerful symbols of immortality to most of our ancestors, who saw freedom in their wings and heaven in their flight. Egyptian, Russian and Irish lore is decorated with promises of becoming a butterfly after death. Aristotle made the word for butterfly and the word for soul, *psyche*, the same in Greek language. The Aztecs and Mayas believed that hummingbirds were the souls of the departed, who returned as comforting companions to the grieving. But whether a butterfly or a hummingbird, ancient cultures nearly always depict the soul as female, deeply in love with Divinity.

From the Song of Solomon in the bible to the Rasa Lila of the Bhagavat Purana, poets of the past lure us toward the sacred with detailed descriptions of amorous dances between the soul and the Divine. Set upon fragrant pastures, or tucked into flowering groves, the ecstatic exchanges are able to speak directly to our human hearts through the language of poetry, regardless of the tradition. It's in this same spirit that the poems in this chapter appear: in equal appreciation of the various diverse religious traditions they represent and the individual hearts from which they poured. For, although their specific visions of the Divine may differ, their poems echo the same sentiments of love, surrender, gratitude and awe, as we hear them enter into a dialogue with the wondrous reality that is beyond us, and yet, simultaneously, within us.

This chapter traces the flight of individual "butterflies" describing the particular type of nectar they taste, as they sip from the flowers of their own individual rituals. We hear them gently land on the petals of traditional religions, in the trumpeting sound of the Jewish *sofar,* the chanting of Sanskrit *mantras* and the breaking of the "Eucharist bread" Inspired by swirling incense and *ashrama* instruments, these spiritual travelers let their souls be as attracted by visions of God wearing a peacock feather in his hair, as they are by Christ's spirit. At other times, they drink from rays of light, assert that the path to divine love is beyond formulas, and have their faith restored by appreciating the sacredness tucked into the ordinary, over a mug of steamy tea. As they spread their pretty wings—each so uniquely colored—perhaps these poets gently remind us that there is food for our souls in every flower, or every tradition, and that exquisite fragrance pours forth when we all gather together, harmoniously, in a spiritual bouquet.

OM

by Jessica Mokrzycki

Sometimes the waves of life seem to pick us up in their fury and heave us upon the jagged rocks that line the shore. They break us into an infinite number of pieces so that we come to a place where we don't even recognize ourselves anymore.

The mystics throughout the world's religions all echo the same sentiment: that in our brokenness if we turn within we can be made whole. That it is when we come to a spiritual state of emptiness and intense longing for truth and God that our hearts are ripe to receive fresh revelation.

I had come to a place of brokenness and longed for some light to seep into my heart, which felt only the bitter sharpness of a darkness so unforgiving and relentless that it was as if my soul was trying to breathe underwater. In these moments of intense longing, like a supernova, a truth so precious and transforming crested the dark mountains adorning the spiritual landscape of my soul. My consciousness was flooded with joy and light. In that moment I realized that what I sought, God, was always with me. In fact, He was closer to me than my very self.

OM

A thousand sighs cannot express
This helpless feeling of brokenness.
Oh Love that stings but no less equips
Give me strength to draw back anger's ships.
Hold these thoughts so very fierce,
Stay the arrow that threatens to pierce
This heart so heavy, sluggish, tired,
This soul needing to be God-inspired.
Flood my bones with joy's true flight.
Employ a thousand waves of light,
Until my parched throat no longer aches,
Until my soul no longer breaks.
Whole again as I've always stood
Now realizing what I always should.
That which is behind sorrow, behind pain,
When all dissipates even the shame,
Left naked and bare at center's core,
Is God; I am no more.
Peace is found when we are zero-
Illusions slain by love's eternal arrow.
I know then that I was never truly broken
For I am one with the first syllable ever spoken.
~Om~

Love is Not a Formula

by Urmila Devi Dasi

Spiritual practices are an entering into a personal relationship of love, and not a mechanical formula. This poem is a reflection on that reality, as I experience it.

Love is Not a Formula

It's not a formula
Oh my dear Madhava!
To push a button
That opens up, then
The world within us
Awake from chrysalis.
It's a dance, my king
Where angels sing
And love perfumes
Heart's inner rooms
How can one make
A way to take
Love, essence of life,
Cut it with a knife
Bottled in a jar
Studied from afar?
Love always resists
An analysis.
Capture is hopeless
And force is useless.
If we want to control,
We remain like a mole
Who desires the sun
While beneath everyone
Digs deep in the ground
And force is useless.

Where the sun is not found
I do not want to love
And need grace from above
For I'm too poor to know
How real love I can show
Can't remember the key
That unlocks the real me.

Fragments of Faith
by Salyna Gracie

It is easy to get lost on the soul's journey. The scope of our task is eclipsed by day-to-day distractions that become detours to doubt. As each new day dawns, we are given the doorway to experiences that renew and revive faith: A quiet morning sitting at my kitchen table, steaming mug of tea in hand, watching the hummingbirds dance at my window helps me to remember my spirit. These small gestures of blessing become the threads that weave faith whole again.

Fragments of Faith

Hope is a welcome guest at my table today
Though these seekers' feet may have stalled
Mired in comforts or complacency   .
I can see the path forward

Eternal intelligences of this body
Its fragility and resilience
Weaving stories of joy and pain
The strength of scars and spirit

Behold the elegance of life
Wonders and artistry moving through
Beauty welling in a broken heart
The majesty and helplessness of loving

There are no secrets in the mirror of remembrance
You are the loom that holds my threads
You are the perfume carried on the breeze
The blessed rhythms of contentment and surrender

On these days when the longing is too great
I find solace in small things
Tiny fragments of faith
That feed my hungry soul

I Know You Are There
by Kia Miller

This poem came through in less than an hour. It speaks of my relationship to the Divine, how our senses can become glorious agents, delivering to us all manner of heavenly delights.

Everything in life is perception. In the Tantric/Kundalini tradition a merging with life is encouraged, rather than withdrawing can we engage wholeheartedly and in doing so, feel every thing as part of one Creative Source represented in a myriad of different ways.

I Know You Are There

I know you are there
I feel you in the longing of my heart
To merge, to become the melody of your song
I see you in the moonlit shimmer on the river,
And the eyes that look back at mine with wild abandon
I hear you as you pluck the strings of my life
and whisper truths in my ears
I taste you in the nectar of sun ripened fruit
and fresh honey comb
I smell you in the fragrance of earth touched by rain,

And the intoxicating scent of Lilies
lavishly revealing their depths
I sense your presence as the carrier of joy and sorrow
The unbiased ever-loving grace of life
The alarm that sounds when I fall unconscious
As the wind that gently tugs at my sleeve
urging me to wake.

Opportunities to Efface My Fear
by Noor-Malika Chishti

I awoke one night and began doing a Sufi practice of remembering God. At one point I had the experience that I did not exist, so who was praying? Fear came into me with this thought and I went into my son's room, woke him up and said, "I just need to make contact real quick then you can go back to sleep."

I have learned that fear in such a situation is a Mercy from God, in that we are protected from expansions for which we are not ready. I turn to the stories of the Prophets and the teachers for inspiration and those influences usually appear in my work. Now, when I meet that place of not existing I am able to breathe into the experience with a little more grace.

Opportunities to Efface My Fear

In facing fear we should remind ourselves
that even Prophets cannot face the Holy Fear
of standing before
the One who causes mountains to crumble.
In the silence of night,
in the depths of Remembrance
my focus was shattered by a glimpse that I did not exist,
... who was saying lâ ilâha illâ allâhu?
A primal fear created by relying on my own deeds

202

closed the door of awareness as a veil of protection.
But, Love of His Beauty is a strong draw
and courage to return is inspired and encouraged by
a message left by one who knew I must
think of the Mercy and Love of my Lord,
give thanks for His Grace
and come without fear.
Did He not promise
that He will Remember me
if I Remember Him?
And, where else should I go but to the heart
for God in His Mercy let us know that is where He can be found.
Early morning is reliable in bringing opportunities to efface my fear
as I strive to create a soul at peace.
I never know when again I might have a chance to not exist and
pray my breath is steady as I release what is not god
into the only One that exists.

Night Calling
by Linda Yael Schiller

I t can be hard to find enough quietness in our lives to be able to hear when we receive a soul-call (our internal hotline to the Divine). It takes several steps to really hear: We first need to stop and hold still, then to pay attention, then to actually listen to the words we hear inside ourselves.

This poem contrasts two types of callings: The loud trumpeting of a *shofar* (ram's horn) which is played on the holy day of Rosh Hashana; *Tekiah* is the name of one of the notes; and is meant as a stirring communal call that none who are present can miss hearing. The other is the reference to the "still small Voice" that the prophet Elijah heard from God in Kings 19:12. God tells Elijah that it is not only in the noise of the thunder and the fire that we can hear God's voice, but also in the deep quiet of our own hearts and minds.

Night Calling

Deep in the hush of the night-cocoon
While the world sleeps
I wake to the call of soft silence.

"Get up" it says-
"Go" it urges:
Listen to this moment.
When the whispered Voice of darkness
Calls your name.

Do not ignore the call.
Shema! Listen!
Not just to the shofar blast of Tekiah
But to this whisper-soft
still small Voice like Elijah heard
Deep within: Calling, calling your name.

Listen to your soul-song
And allow your soul to resonate
With the shiver of the strings
plucked by the Source
of the music of the stars.

As a finely tuned violin also sounds
when another is played nearby.

Follow that sound as you take your soul's journey
To this place/time
That is both now and then.

Blue Prayer

by Salyna Gracie

How often we lay awake in the depth of night with a longing we cannot place. In those moments when the veil between worlds thins, we reach for our Beloved: The Divine Spirit that lives in those we love and within ourselves.

In the stillness, we may ache for a far away friend or mourn the loss of one we have loved. Or maybe we reach, yet again, for the small being that depends on us for every comfort. And always, we pray for the strength to continue loving.

Blue Prayer

In the deep contracted night
Again, I reach for you
Arms outstretched
Fingers taut
This meager embrace
Worn and weary

I reach between worlds
With my only heart
Its four-quartered arrow
Pierces the sleepless air
Tender and fierce
Like courage
Like hope
Like love

Prayer

by Ruth Calder Murphy

"The Dance" has become for me a metaphor for life —For existence as a whole, in fact, where Life includes our physical deaths and whatever might lie beyond them. Many of my poems refer to the Dance, or dancing, because for me, "The Dance" is a metaphor for life and my poetry is the way I express it.

This poem, Prayer, is saying something that's at the core of my perspective. Firstly, that prayer, worship, connection with the Divine, is not only about one-off rituals or events, but about the whole of life, our whole experience of *living*. It's what the Dance is all about.

Secondly, that everything we are, everything - and everyone - we see or hear or touch, in whatever way, is an expression of that Divinity. We, and the world around us, *are* the Dance and the Dance itself IS Divine.

Prayer

I will dance the dance of the ocean.
I will dance the dance of the trees.
I will dance with the surf-capped waves
and the breeze-crazed leaves.
I will dance the dance of the meadow,
the dance of the mountaintops,
I will dance with the blood-red poppies
and the lichened rocks.
I will dance the dance of moonlight,
I will dance where sunbeams play;
I will dance with the stars at midnight
and with the golden day.
I will dance the dance of living,
I will dance the dance of prayer.
I will dance to the dancing centre
and meet you there.

Gratitude

by Rev. Doris Davis

This poem was written after my daughter, Viveka and I had just completed our cross-country American mother-daughter walkabout. We were attending a weeklong seminar in Oak Park IL on "Sacred Activism." These words flowed out after a meditation.

Gratitude

In the secret chamber of the heart
some words arose that took the form of prayer.
Around the space four presences were gathered:
the one who always presides, and the witness,
and the two -- the body and the soul.

The soul addressed the body and said:
"Beloved one, you honor me today,
leaving all burdens of the past behind,
forgiving me and letting yourself be forgiven.
Only gratitude is left in the space between us.
Give me your hand, and let us celebrate
what G-d has given us to know of Love."

At Her Eucharist

by Becky Crigger

This poem was written in honor of an Episcopal priest and mystic. On the last day of a week-long Wisdom School in Valle Crucis, North Carolina, we celebrated the Eucharist in an apple barn. Our time there was modeled after the Benedictine Monastic order, and we spent it praying and working alone and together and honoring the sacred silence in the evenings. The retreat center was formerly the very first Anglican monastery in the US.

At Her Eucharist

Her grey rugged clothes and navy cap
Invite me into priestly authenticity.
There are no robes here tonight
No stained glass or pews.
Just a dimly lit red barn at the bottom of a hill,
A circle of chairs framing a small wooden table
Set with bread and wine, body and blood.
A drum and singing bowl, small bouquet of flowers.

Her hardened hands circle the cup
Calling me to this gift
Asking me to be emptied, to be ready."
Leave all things that you have,
Come and follow me."
The drum is quiet as we stand,
Grows louder as we turn.
Turning and turning, backwards in time.

She holds the bread and speaks to us.
What is this language as we prepare the feast?
A conversation, not a creed
An intimacy, not a routine.
My legs begin to shake as one by one
We make our way to her table
Taking the bread, breaking it in our hands
Lifting the cup, drinking it in our time.

I feel the tears warm my face
As my knees graze the dusty floor,
My interlaced fingers trembling
As I imagine Saint Teresa on the stone

Weeping in her newfound devotion.
In the stillness the moment ceases.
Time is all, all is time.
He is here.

Pregnant Pause

by Sarah Courtney Dean

This poem was written in the month of July just as the day was dawning and it describes what I experienced that morning so well: an experience that reflects my Druid belief that the Divine is in everything. And I could certainly feel Her that morning!

Pregnant Pause

There is a silence over everything today
As if the earth is pregnant.
Broken by the buzz of bees
Hovering from flower to flower
Feverishly trying to outrun
The coming storm.
The air is heavy with a fecund smell
And dripping moisture
Like Angels weeping tears of joy for creation.
Soon though the storm will break
And the tears become a flood
And the silence broken
By thunderbolts from the Gods.

The Way of Birth

by Jennifer Hawley-Zechlin

In many spiritual traditions the mythologies of creation and destruction are woven together, each being dependent on the other: Birth, death, and resurrection create cycles of eternity, each incomplete without the other.

In the poem The Way of Birth, I explore some of these symbols whilst at the same time honoring the process within myself, which can often be painful. Pain is present in endings - whether it comes as the end of a relationship, a child getting ready to head out on their own, or even as the taming of our own selves.

Whatever the destruction, it's important for me to remember that creation and newness comes on painful heels. The Way of Birth is the way of life.

The Way of Birth

The Universe has been pregnant with us
for a very long time now,
You and I.
We have been together, united but separate,
Growing in Universe-Utero.
You, a fetus awaiting all the good things to come;
Sunshine warm on your thin pale face,
Diamond studded sand for your bare feet to walk on
Leaving golden glitter between your toes,
The music of birdsong in the morning as you rise
and whispering breezes to lull-a-bye you at night.
I have been your placenta.
I have sheltered you and protected you,
delivered nourishment from the Womb of All Life,
and allowed you to expel your waste.
Through me.
I have not been your life-source.

Your birth is not dependent on me.
And yet, without me, you would never make it to life
Free to breathe for the first time
Sweet, luscious air scented by lilacs
and Summer heat.
I, though so very different from you,
would not have existed without you.
I never would have plumped up,
Crimson-Purple, filled with life,
Clinging passionately to the Universe's Uterus.
Without you, without us, both awaiting birth,
I never would have become feeder.
Maybe that's where we made our mistake,
You and I.
Perhaps, like an overdue infant,
we became too comfortable in that
dark
silent
confining Womb.
taking each other for granted
and refusing to feel the pains of labour.
Still, labour will come. Birth can not be avoided.
The pains have already begun.
I have already begun to tear away from our shared Womb's wall.
I can provide you no more,
and though it will be frightening and a little violent
(Because birthing is always a little violent),
soon you will be born.
Do not fear, my love.
When it is over, you will be able to rest
Safe in the arms of your Mother.
You will grow and toddle and live.
And I too will be birthed.
Tearing away completely and making the same journey you do.
Separate,
and ready to enter the Universe and be transformed.
For this is the way of birth.
For both you and I.

Winged Secret

by Arna Baartz

I love poetry and art! They are the two ways I get to express the deep, abiding knowingness that we are all one: One creature pulsing to the music of the universe, participating in a story of individuality and separation.

My poem 'winged secret' is a remembering of our oneness, an exploration into the connection between the physical and the spiritual... the reminder in fact that these two things are not separate at all.

Winged Secret

it is beating
in me
this winged secret
this blue gold illusion
pulsing a no time mathematics
spreading like jasmine oil
flowing musical
de vivre
de joi
I AM
earth nuzzled
and heaven bound
coiled
with mystical sound
sweet sensuality
and forever
revolving
dissolving....

Be Coming

by Kai Coggin

We are all on a Journey to reach our Highest Self: the Self that knows and sees all things, the Self that is Holy among the Holy, the Self that originates from the Central Sun, the Self that is inside us all.

This poem is about seeing the journey for what it is, letting go of attachment, and calling out to the others that I see on my path who are speaking from their Souls. May we recognize our joined Spirits striving towards the goal of being truly free!

Be Coming

Hold all my aching and growing,
make your body a vessel
for everything I have to fill you,
it may not be much
but it might just be everything.

I have heard the soul is shaped like a bowl
a reversed dome of the Heavens,
we are golden receptors of beauty,
magnets that pull stars into our lowest points
until they build towers of light
from our sternums.

Rise and fall chest,
metronomic movement of body
keeping time for the sages,
inside me a heart breathing
sound of lullabies for sleeping angels,
Great Servers
who wear gravity like a badge of honor,
like a gown of trees rooted in earth,

wake up, my friends,
hold my hand through this;
I think I know the way,
otherwise, my true north tongue
will hasten into Mercury-mouthed
stutters of half truths
and I will taste the metal compass spin,
follow my fallen sparred-off feathers
to the gates of your own becoming,
Be coming,
Be going back to that body of light
that birthed you like a sun into space,
the plasma of dreams,
the expectancy of orbits,
the nomenclature of God, who has a thousand names

All of them being You.
All of them being Me.

Our Abundant Mother: The Universe

by Chemutai Sigei

I wrote these poems as a celebration: as offerings of gratitude to The Universe as I experience it. They are in tune with the style of the oral traditions of Swahili poetry from Kenya, East Africa, where I come from.

The first poem came one morning as I was taking a walk along a beautiful pond near my home. I was struck by a wondrous experience of the glorious universe before and within me. Feeling the words flow from my heart, I wrote them down on my phone as I sat beside a beautiful pond.

The second poem is what emerged from my heart as I was meditating on peace and kindness towards others, reflecting on the way we experience this life on earth.

Our Abundant Mother: The Universe

How can we thank our abundant Mother, The Universe?
She gives and sustains life in her womb
She provides us with air to breathe
She silently toils and yields more than we can consume
She gives us light and clothes us with warmth
She gives and gives without a break
All, abounds in greatest measures
How can we thank our abundant Mother, The Universe?

Soft, Gentle And Yet Deep Steps

Oh I wish everyone's steps were soft as petals here on earth:
Light and yet deep in depth
Gentle with a likeness of baby's first steps
And beautiful like prints of flowers
Remember, your steps manifest that which is high
Oh! I wish they would be the gentlest steps
Which bring peace, love, joy and happiness to all on earth.

Cruel Senseless Things
by Sharon Gannon

I was reading the commentary on a passage in the Bhagavad Gita, by a respected guru that said, "All living entities can be divided into two divisions: those that can move and those that are stationary, such as trees." I felt disheartened by this statement and much of what was written in the book after that, because to me it reflected a speciesistic and misogynistic view as well as a generally negative view of nature.

It seems like we have deluded ourselves for so long that most of us believe that men are the crown of creation. Prejudice can be a strong disease that eats away from the inside out, like a virus that is able to disguise itself and appear as being the same as its host.

Thank God, these prejudices are not hard-wired in us—they are learned and what is learned can be unlearned. I believe that it is possible that we can wake up from our ignorant delusion and see the world through enlightened eyes of wonderous compassion. When we do we will recognize that all of life is alive, animated by the living love of God. This poem is a call to awaken!

Cruel Senseless Things

Who says trees can't walk
And birds can't talk
And fishes are cold blooded
Cruel Senseless things

Who says rocks don't smell
And pigs can't tell
And fishes are cold blooded
Cruel senseless things

Who says rivers don't die
And flowers can't lie
And fishes are cold blooded
Cruel senseless things

Who says that only men are people
Endowed with souls, minds and
Feelings, who can think, speak,
reflect, remember and aspire
While all the rest
Are dumb and stupid
Put here to be acquired
As if we were separate
From the world
And that the world would be a

Better place if only men
Inhabited every space

They say fishes are cold blooded
Cruel senseless things
But what about a man
Who says such things?

Imagine
by Ruth Calder Murphy

Amongst others, there is a certain passage in the Bible that gives me goose bumps. It seems to whisper something bigger than I can quite put my finger on. It's in the New Testament Letter to the Ephesians and is talking about being able to approach God with confidence... It goes on to say:

> "For this reason I kneel before the Father, from whom every family in heaven and on earth derives its name. I pray that out of his glorious riches he may strengthen you with power through his Spirit in your inner being, so that Christ may dwell in your hearts through faith. And I pray that you, being rooted and established in love, may have power, together with all the Lord's holy people, to grasp how wide and long and high and deep is the love of Christ, and to know this love that surpasses knowledge—that you may be filled to the measure of all the fullness of God. Now to him who is able to do immeasurably more than all we ask or imagine, according to his power that is at work within us, to him be glory in the church and in Christ Jesus throughout all generations, for ever and ever!"

This stirs something deep inside me: the idea that we're all joined in Divine love. That we have divinity - Spirit - in the very core of our beings and that, in this strength, this power at work in us, all is possibility. Beyond what we imagine, beyond what we ask - more than our human minds can grasp.

As a Panentheist, I see Divinity manifested in all things - the earth, the moon, the stars, other human beings, my self... And it is there - it's here - that immeasurable power is at work - all through being rooted and established in Love, because God - or Goddess - Divinity, is Love.

Imagine

Beyond what I ask
or imagine,
is Possibility.

I imagine my soul,
a deep-rooted,
branch-stretching tree,
balanced between the rich earth
and the infinite sky,
reaching to eternity;
beyond Now,
beyond I...

I imagine the moon in my belly
and the moon bearing me,
reflecting sunshine
in silvered silence
and riding the starry sky
til dawn...

I imagine my spirit,
singing with stars
in spiraling galaxies,
turning towards infinity,
towards eternity,
towards home...

I ask that my song be beautiful
and true,
star-bright,
ancient,
ever-new,
echoing in everything
and belling to Beyond...

Beyond what I ask,
beyond what I imagine...
and then,
in perpetuity,
Possibility.

You Found Me

by Maira de La Cruz

I began to relish expressing my thoughts on paper one summer night while residing in the holy city of Vrindavan, India. I had been writing before in the U.S. but it was different there; I would write for my own self. I considered my writings to be very private and was always very hesitant to share my real self.

While traveling India I began to feel inspired, surrounded by so much spiritual beauty. I heard a voice from within urging me to stop being so selfish to share the love I felt for God: Krishna, the beloved of the Gopis in Vraj, who found me and called me back towards him!

My life has changed completely into a joyful one, and positive energy has been flowing through my veins from the very beginning of my new life in *bhakti* yoga. In this poem I glorify and express my gratitude towards Krishna for bringing me back to life.

You Found Me

I am found!
No longer lost in the concrete jungle of the world.
I see the fresh path that is true and green.

Thus, I sing to you with cymbals of gratitude
and drums that beat your love and glories
into the hearts of the sincere.

Love.
Like a giant wave that crashes...
Plundering and purifying...
Inundating the city of nine gates
where the soul lies asleep.

Wake up sleeping souls!
Stop dreaming up illusions!

No time to waste.
Time is life. Time is death.

The divine sun that is your soul within
wishes to rise above the dark clouds of ignorance.

Blazing light.
Smiling rays.
I see truth.

I Hold You, Torah

by Ruth Broyde Sharone

As a Jewish woman and conscious inheritor of the legacy of the feminist movement in America, I have been able to do what many

Jewish women in the world still cannot do: hold the Torah, my sacred scripture, in my arms. In the majority of Orthodox communities, women are not permitted to hold the Torah and they cannot be ordained as Rabbis--at least not yet.

While making the film "Today I Am A Rabbi," I had a profound and stirring experience. I was documenting three women, all in their 50's, who became the first graduates of the Academy for Jewish Religion (AJR) in Los Angeles.

I remember the ecstatic look on the face of Rabbi Tsipora Gabai, when she was ordained as the first Moroccan-born female Rabbi in the world, breaking the gender taboo after nine consecutive generations of male Rabbis in her family. Tears glistened in the eyes of Rabbi Alicia Magal as she lovingly enveloped the Torah in her arms, and we all heard the tremor in the voice of Rabbi Miriam Hamrell as she confessed to the audience how all her life she had longed to hold the Torah, but tradition had prevented it.

The film I made was a conscious ode to women spiritual leaders everywhere, but it also was dedicated specifically to Jewish women who aspire to get closer to the Torah and become full partners in celebrating Judaism alongside of Jewish men. The poem, however, was not about equality of men and women in religious life. Instead it reflected my personal realization at how challenging it can be--even as I was clinging to the physical Torah in my arms--to embody and integrate Jewish wisdom into my life. One's commitment to that embodiment becomes a daily decision, at times a welcome one and at times too heavy to bear... until the next moment when we may get to experience the "sweet lightness of being."

I Hold You, Torah

Nestled in my eager arms,
your soft velvet robe against my cheek,
your short legs supported in my lap,
like my own babies, not so long ago,

221

I sense the longing we all have felt
my sisters and I,
our mothers and grandmothers and their mothers before them,
to hold you, Torah
to know you, Torah
to feel your wisdom as close as our breath.

You are our locus, Torah, our history and our future.
You are our desert guide,
our North Star in the moonless sky.
Your yellow wizened skin bares the evidence of Ha-Shem,
the holy words that formed us and brought us to this day.
Your elegant script ascends and descends, in chapter and verse,
carrying us on eagle wings
to our refuge and our salvation.

Your melody is the bittersweet music of our ancestors,
curse and blessing,
drum and flute,
despair and jubilation,
harp and tambor.
I hold you, Torah
I know you, Torah
I feel your wisdom as close as my breath

As I bask in your strength,
hoping this intimate moment will never end,
slowly I become aware of a rising discomfort.
How much effort it takes to hold you tight, Torah,
to support your insistent wooden legs,
now heavy in my lap.
I try to find a place of ease.
It is no use.
You have become a burden.

How long must I hold you so tight, Torah?
How long must I support you
to make sure you will not fall?

My delight has become dismay, my joy an ordeal.
Is there no time to rest from this yoke?
No respite? No relief?
How difficult it has become
To hold you, Torah
To know you, Torah,
To feel your wisdom as close as my breath.

My arms ache
My shoulders sag
I am weary from the effort.
I want to release you and not feel guilt.
I shift my legs back and forth
to ease the pressure I feel.
But there is no easy place I can find
without feeling your demands.

Why did I take on this task, Torah?
Why did I commit to this responsibility?
How could I have foreseen the difficulties
To hold you, Torah
To know you, Torah
To feel your wisdom as close as my breath.

And then, just as slowly,
Without warning,
I watch my discomfort slide away.
My tired arms feel new strength
as they encircle you and
draw you even closer to my heart.
My lap accommodates the pressure
of your powerful legs
For they have found the perfect resting place.

The softness of your blue velvet robe
comforts my cheek
I hear the melody of your scripture
in my innermost ear.

I taste your love for all of us
on my lips
and in the meditations of my heart.

I hold you, Torah
I know you, Torah
I feel your wisdom as close as my breath.

Love's Sweet Nectar

by Jessica Mokrzycki

There is something so holy and precious regarding the names of God. Upon every tongue in every corner of the world vibrations in praise of a God who is universal rise up in devotion. The names might differ, but they are all directed towards the same reality: Recognition of the Eternal.

I have found that in my case the names of God found in the *maha-mantra* draw my heart deeper into a realization of God and His infinite nature and begin to connect me to His love and towards the desire to serve and surrender to Him.

Like an arrow, my mantra has buried itself deep within me. It's as if an underground spring of freshly flowing water from eternity itself has been struck and now passes through me, nourishing my parched soul with its transcendental nectar.

I wrote the following poem after I had chanted several rounds of my *mantra* on my *japa mala* beads and went outside to walk our border collie in the gently falling rain.

I now no longer chanted but sang the names of God to whoever was around to hear: the neighbor's cat stalking moths and crickets across our back lawn, the trees with their outstretched arms glistening wet. And it was if my heart took flight and began dancing along with the raindrops that fell. As they fell nourishing the earth something within me overflowed nourishing my soul. When I came inside I tried to put my thoughts and feelings in a poem and this poem was the result.

Love's Sweet Nectar

When love washes away all pain,
When knowing God is your only gain,
When His mercy removes illusion's stain;
Your soul learns to dance with the rain.

There is no greater feeling than This-
Being held by the hands of Eternal Bliss.
The nectar is so sweet to taste,
You run into His arms in all haste.

Hare Krishna Hare Krishna, Krishna Krishna Hare Hare
Hare Rama Hare Rama, Rama Rama Hare Hare

When he holds you in His hands
And whispers to you of greater lands;
Those woven by His higher energy
Where from the material one is finally free.

When He says, yes this child is mine,
And His peace washes over you sublime;
Your inner heart kneels before His presence within,
The mundane becomes just background din.

True freedom is conceived from a soul who surrenders,
To hearts devoted to Him, His Mercy He renders.
Everything we need is in His holy names
They lead us back to Him from where we first came.

Hare Krishna Hare Krishna, Krishna Krishna Hare Hare
Hare Rama Hare Rama, Rama Rama Hare Hare

Divine Visitation

by Radha Dasi Cornia

This poem came to me after I had a very special dream about Madhana. Madhana is a name of God that refers to Divine Love in the bhakti yoga tradition I belong to.

Divine Visitation

My dreaming eyes beheld a room swept bare
Of all the clutter from my waking hours
White walls and wooden floors encountered there
And the fragrance of night blooming jasmine flowers
Sunlight broke through on the windowsill
Then danced upon the walls like golden lace
I saw the sunlight and my heart grew still
Enraptured by the quiet of that place
All at once I felt a presence there
I heard a footstep brush across the floor
Like peacock feathers soft upon the stair
Then sweet Madhana entered at my door
Illuminated like the sky at dawn
When all the world is rendered fresh and clear
My heart grew lighter as I gazed upon
The beauty of His face as He drew near
Clothed in honey silk and tawny pearls
Garland made of Tulsi and of rose
Pink as the blushing cheeks of maiden girls
Who could not be lovelier in His clothes
Black hair caressed His cheeks and caught the light
Reflected from His luminescent face
I felt my body tremble at the sight
I prayed I might surrender to His grace
Then fell before Him on the wooden floor
Tempted by the shelter of His feet

The fragrance of the flowers that he wore
Was intoxicating, mystically sweet.
He smiled and my head began to reel
Inebriated by one sacred glance
That loosed my grip on Maya Devi's wheel
As I yielded to celestial romance
But tears were in my eyes when I awoke
Grieving for a treasure that is lost
I cannot recall the words He spoke
And in my waking world I pay the cost
Let me gratefully forgo the morning sun
Eternally renounce my waking role
Content if I can only gaze upon
That ethereal seducer of my soul

Murali Vadana

by Madhava Lata Dasi

At the age of eighteen I traveled from my home in Italy to India on a personal spiritual search. My journey ended in an ashram in Vrindavan. The early nights in the ashram were long, hot and humid. But they became tolerable by the mesmerizing sound of Veena singing. I loved sitting in her room listening to her poetic songs.

Once, Veena taught me how to write a poem: She asked me to visualize an emotion and consider how to express it in words. So I started writing. From them on whenever I felt impelled to write my realizations, or feelings, or emotions, it was natural for me to express it through poetry.

To me, poetry is the language of the soul on this long path to surrender and to love. As a practitioner of *bhakti* yoga, I need to cultivate a soft heart. Poetry helps me greatly in this sense. I was taught that in *bhakti* yoga the ultimate goal is to "never forget Krishna", so my poetry is mostly about Krishna, or God.

My poem is called Murali Vandana, which is a name for Krishna when he holds the flute to His lips, stealing the minds and hearts of his devotees with his enchanting melodies. My poem is about God's longing for souls. Especially his beloved Radha, the Queen of Vraja: that wonderful place where every breeze, every season, every horizon and every landscape become fuel for Krishna's amorous heart. In Krishna's lonesome reminiscing of Radha's love for him, he plays his flute, calling her, and all of us, back to his divine sweetness. The book Gopala Champu by Jiva Goswami inspired this poem.

Murali Vandana

In the taste of water
is Krishna,
His blue skinmirrors
His infinityin the oceans
and in the enveloping skies
for all rests in Him,
while in His mind
dwells beauty, pleasure and rasa,
but only in Vraja
His love thickens
and His blue hue deepens
as a swollen rainy cloud,
and only there
His flute, in an enchanting sound,
brings about the autumn
of playful breezes,
and on an inviting note
agitating the minds
He calls to dance
under the moonlight
and a festival of scales,
tunes, tones, tinkling and trills
captures the hands, the bodies and the feet.

But this eons-long night of rasa
seems to vanish
in one note of His raga,
and when the horizon swallows
His nocturnal secrecy of mellows,
still inebriated of pleasure,
He gazes at the peeping light
and by the beauty
of His lotus petal-like eyes
blends of pink
the dawn of sleepless night.
And once alone, aloof,
Up there, on the devoted Hill
pensively, standing
shaded by the tree,
He remembers the White Lotus
whirling, adorned by a moonbeam,
oozing a fragrant dew
Of shiny drops.
And when caressed softly,
by the cooling petal of His hand
slipped like pearls between His fingers,
where now the notes of His flute linger
giving away His thoughts
in soulful melodic strains
of His longing
for meeting Radha once again.

The Poetry of Devotion

by Braja Sorensen

Every temple, mosque, cathedral, chapel, abbey, basilica, or church is special...the older it is, the more it has seen, the more glorification of the Supreme Lord it has heard, the more prayers its walls have absorbed. These are special, holy places, sacred sites, ancient memorials often witnessing centuries of devotion!

These buildings aren't stagnant: they have life, they hold memories, they share secrets...their scent is intoxicating, the resounding voices of praise that travel around their walls irreplaceable, the softness of their age, a shelter. We enter with awe, with reverence, with wonder, curiosity, love, pain, and a beseeching heart. We stand, go on bended knee, lie in obeisance...and we listen...

The Poetry of Devotion

"If these walls could speak..." but they do;
Words uttered through eternity
Whispering beauty softly spoken
Poetry in stone.

What wisdom, sunk into these walls?
"Lean closer," they say. "We will tell
of sages old, mantras chanted."
Poetry in song.

What tales in smoke of frankincense?
Exotic, the perfume of time
perspires from pores of ancient stone
Poetry in scent.

Humble presence, the marble floor
Worn soft and smooth by the faithful
Slow forging of paths trod with love
Poetry in motion.

Rapturous notes, song of the heart
Echoing through the centuries
Continual cycle of words
Poetry in devotion.

Timeless elements combine, an
eternal poetic embrace

All for the pleasure of the Lord;
Poetry of love.

"If these walls could speak," and they do —
of eternal devotion, prayer,
timeless acts of love
Poetry of eternity.

Afterword
Pinching at Poetry

"Everywhere I go I find that a poet has been there before me."
Sigmund Freud

The year I turned thirteen poems began trickling out of me like drips out of a leaky dam. My poems were born of loneliness and were the orphans of the country I'd left behind. Their cries would send me to the eucalyptus grove across the street from our house -writing tablet and pen in hand- to catch the desperate sound of sea breezes rustling through leaves before sunset.

It seems I was becoming Kierkegaard's definition of a poet: an anguished heart whose cries sounded like music. My songs of solitude started with an enumerated series of short poems that were nearly haiku-like, called, simply, 'The Tree'. They all had begun with light, ended with darkness, and with the brush strokes of a naturalist, painted simple psychological portraits of the parts of me that needed the most attention. So I disguised my feelings as bark, and roots, and trunks that swayed in powerful gales threatening to break them, and leafs that were always falling.

In the years after we abruptly left my childhood home, every time I felt alone and unheard I poured myself into a poem. This filled me with such addictive satisfaction that by the time I was sixteen my trickle of poems had turned into the fierce waters rushing from a broken dam after a record-breaking rainfall.

I scribbled poems in school when I should have been listening to the teacher. I spent many school lunches in the library, looking for quiet corners that would feed my compositions. I wrote on the bus ride home from school, and in my room after school, and in the middle of the night when I couldn't sleep. I wrote with such intensity that my finger grew a little bunion where the pen rested. Today, that little bump on my finger stands as an endearing testament to how poetry created a firm passage for me to walk upon when I felt like all other ground under me was crumbling.

The poems I wrote as a teenager were, for the most part, not pretty poems. They were laden with achiness, and prickly perspectives, and itchy feelings their readers needed to shake off as soon as possible. My poems were raw, jagged-edged emotional outpourings that hit the page at a hundred miles an hour independently of any rules or mentors, splashing in all kinds of uncomfortable directions. They morphed into studies of my pain and inevitably became screeches to my mother —as any mother would cringe upon discovering that her baby is hurting- and music to my shrink!

But to me, my poems were my emancipators, galloping down hills of adolescent turbulence with shiny swords raised and wild manes blowing in the wind. My poems even made my depression look beautiful! I think Shelley was most fond of that function of poetry: its ability to infuse even the ugliest of subjects with beauty. Framed in poetry, the unapproachable suddenly becomes approachable.

Poetry seems to get away with successfully presenting what others might find objectionable in prose. Its playful use of words makes it language's endearing child delightfully beyond reproach. I took full advantage of this and never limited what topics I explored in my poems. Reservations dissolve when intoxicated with the exhilarating process of pouring oneself into a poem.

I wouldn't say that my adolescent poetry was good by any literary standards, as no one ever taught me about meter, rhyming, diction or alliteration. I was never formally educated in poetry composition. But form proved secondary to me when substance reigned supreme, for my relationship to my poems was utilitarian: they were my brave liberators. They were fearless explorers of uncharted terrain. My poems were the wild and uneducated swings of an intuitive machete as it blazed trails through the existential jungle of my adolescence.

So, as a teenager, I wrote poems to flirt with boundaries of where I begun and where I ended. I used them to deconstruct myself and carefully stitch myself back together again. Like patchwork on a quilt,

I wove many sides of myself into a singular poem. Each poem was like a code, which, if deciphered, opened windows into places I wanted to explore: landscapes of my being. The process of composition doubled as an adventure in self-discovery. Sometimes the journey was terrifying, as I scratched at words and pinched at sonnets, looking for myself, to the tune of individuation.

Like an underground river, my writing of poems disappeared as I exited that period of my life. And yet, though poems no longer rushed *from me*, they continued to swirl *in me*, as poetry had permanently inundated my being.

Robert Frost once described being a poet as an unshakable 'condition'. Thus, being a poet is not only what happens when one splashes words on paper: it's a continual *state of being*. Poets view the unfolding of life itself as a poem. As I experience it, being a poet is a heighted sensitivity. It's a continual dialogue with nature: inner and outer. Poetry is what spontaneously injects perspective with metaphor even as one washes the dishes, weeds the garden, stuffs kale into a juicer or scrubs the bathroom tiles. Consequently, I noticed that some of my best poetry gets written when I'm showering or doing dishes, and not when I am sitting at my laptop.

I am tempted to say that at a certain point poetry simply merges with one's very essence. Voltaire called poetry "the music of the soul, and, above all, of great and feeling souls." I believe that if we excavate deeply inside ourselves, we all eventually hit poetry's treasure chest. There are poetic gems to be mined, if only we let ourselves be used as the tools that will do so.

For poetry to flow a yielding stance is required. To the Greeks, poetic skill was synonymous with becoming open and receptive to the celestial muse Polyhymnia. Many ancient cultures believed that poets yielded to the divinities, and were thus able to speak in their language. All Sanskrit verse, for example, is regarded as a passage to the sacred, for poetry weds words to sound, and —according to quantum physics-sound threads connect us all at a subatomic level.

This sonic oneness was poetically expressed across cultures and throughout history, as the sharing of poetry has an oral origin. As a child who simply *adored* the Museum of Anthropology in Mexico City, I loved imagining tribes gathering around fires to ingest poetry, drumming out in exciting rhythms matching the beats in nature, and syncopated with the thumps in a listener's chest.

As I experience it, the process of gestating a poem in me certainly plays with my heartbeat. I can definitely feel a poem in my body first before it emerges. Poems grow in my core, and kick right before they are ready to come out. Sometimes birthing them hurts. Robert Frost once wrote that a poem begins with a lump in the throat. And once it's born, a poem takes on its own life! Poetry makes its way into the lives of readers through books salvaged at yard sales, readings in cozy coffeehouses, blogs that others accidentally stumble upon, posts on Facebook. The mischief they get into after that is a subjective affair.

Leonardo da Vinci paralleled the enjoyment of poetry with experiencing a painting that is felt rather than seen. Writing poetry was like that for me in my teen years: a form of expression that teetered between painting and prose. I used to oscillate between the two, and when neither medium was equipped enough to hold me (and all my complexity), poetry worked every time. Consequently, I filled whole journals with my poems. It was an emotional purging of sorts. When I was done I had created a beautiful new life for myself, and my poetry went into hibernation.

It wasn't until that life began to crumble, over a decade later, that I started writing poetry again. Picasso once said that: "Every act of creation is first an act of destruction". As life around me began to fall, my poems, predictably, began to rise again: like little suns shining the way, in synch with my own intuition. And my poetry blazed through outdated images of my self in a frenzy of reinvention. It was the good kind of destruction that erupts in colorful flames and dances wildly like Lord Shiva, burning soil to provide nourishment for the next seeds.

Audre Lorde spoke of poetry as that which *"lays the foundations for a future of change, a bridge across our fears of what has never been before."* When my first marriage began to evaporate, I built such bridges in secret, wriggling in a cocoon of transformation from which I finally emerged ten years later. My poems weren't reproducing like rabbits as they did before, but the process of writing them was powerful, and it became a kind of companion to me: the kind that holds a mirror up to you. It was a visceral journey that reached toward spirit.

So, making poetry took me and shook me, and unexpectedly reminded me of beauty I had misplaced. It also discarded a few stagnating parts of me I later tossed into coffins and happily erected gravestones to. For, sometimes poems resemble epitaphs and sometimes they twitch like fresh butterfly wings drying in the sun. As for me, after much twitching, I think my wings are finally beginning to dry now.

For women...poetry is not a luxury. It is a vital necessity of our existence. It forms the quality of the light within which we predicate our hopes and dreams...It lays the foundations for a future of change, a bridge across our fears of what has never been before.

Audre Lorde

A Glimpse into The Authors

Vrinda Aguilera is a Montessori trained primary school teacher, an intuitive energy healer, a poet, and practitioner of Bhakti yoga. She is passionate about supporting women on their spiritual journey. She lives in rural Florida with her husband and three children where she blossoms in the experience of being a mother.

Sandra Allagapen is originally from Mauritius but now lives in London where accountancy, healing therapies, jewelry making and poetry are some of the colors on the palette of her life. She dreams of spending more time in Italy one day and loves books, crystals and long summer evenings. Contact Sandra at www.empoweredheart.co.uk

Nancy Alder is a mom, yoga teacher and writer. She teaches the Yoga of Ease through awareness of anatomy, acceptance and humor. Nancy's writing has been featured in Origin Magazine and Mantra Yoga + Health Magazine where she is also an editor. You can find her off her mat at www.flyingyogini.com

Cassandra Alls, known to many as the HOLISTIC DIVA, is an organic goddess, soldier of love, healer, giver, plant-based foodie, artist, yogi, activist, writer, traveler, rebel, and spiritual junkie. She has published two works of poetry. Follow her bliss at www.holisticdiva.com

Kiernan Antares is an artist, poet, and *yogini* whose journey has taken her down many paths; as a spiritual healer, teacher, mystic, author, radio show host. She now rests in the path of the Beauty Way through artistic expression, celebrating the Divine Feminine and inspiring women to awaken the inner Goddess.

Helene Averous is a mother who has found peace in the depth of the heart after an intense self-inquiry. Her journey transformed her from an active executive woman to the author of picture books for kids about colors and a mystic/Zen poetry book, "Silent Drops". More info on www.heleneaverous.com.

Arna Baartz is mother to eight beautiful children, a poet, visual artist and educator living in Australia. Connect with her and her work at arnabaartz.com. There you will find links to Silver Poetry and The I AM Program (emotional intelligence resources for children). You may also follow her on twitter or Facebook.

Andréa Balt is a writer, blogger, creativity curator & wellness alchemist living in Spain. She is also co-founder and editor-in-chief of RebelleSociety.com and co-creator of RebelleWellness.com. Find her latest writing on AndreaBalt.com, and connect with her on Facebook & Twitter @andreabalt or via Instagram@creativerehab

Ginny Brannan resides in Massachusetts with her husband, son and two cats. Encouraged by her best friend, she started writing poetry in 2009. She enjoys writing in both form and free verse, and her work has been published in The dVerse Anthology available at Amazon.com Find her poetry at http://insideoutpoetry.blogspot.com

Anita Brown is a mom/poet/yoga instructor in pursuit of becoming the woman God created. She loves walking her golden retriever, Sierra, in the park, where she is inspired by nature's beauty. Never one to shy away from a new opportunity, she has been teaching yoga and meditation to underserved populations, including the incarcerated.

Del-Rita Butler is living in the light as a conscious choice. She believes that love *Changes* the world and that it only takes **One** individual to ignite *Change*. She sees each one of us as an instrument of peace, love, and light. Her poetry encourages us to ask ourselves who we are when no one is watching, and to self-evaluate, and change.

Nancy Carlson writes poems as insight, healing, expression of love and devotion to the Divine. Living in Boston, she works as an RN, Health, Wellness and Life Purpose Coach, Reiki Master and Yoga Teacher. Always curious, she enjoys studying Ayurveda, reading sacred texts, hiking, deep conversations, creating, cooking, and community. Contact her via Facebook.

Andreja Cepus is a Social Artist from Slovenia, Europe. After working for several years in the marketing & communications field, she is now fully dedicated to serve through creative communications, hosting and facilitating workshops, spiritual traveling and art inspirational events that are uniting different fields and reawakening divine feminine principle in our society. Visit her website at social-artist.si.

Noor-Malika Chishti has been a student in the Sufi tradition since 1972 and serves as a Representative of Pir Zia Inayat Khan, President of the Sufi Order International. Board member for reGeneration, founding member Greater LA Muslim-Jewish Solidarity Committee. Noor-Malika has presented in interfaith conferences internationally. She is a Grandmother.

Kai Coggin is a full-time poet and freelance writer born in Bangkok and living in AR. She holds a Bachelor of Arts in Poetry and Creative Writing from Texas A&M University. Kai has been published in various journals and released her first chapbook, In Other Words, in August 2013. Kai is now seeking publication of her first full-length manuscript, PERISCOPE HEART.

Pranada Comtois is a spiritual activist passionate about embodying, and writing about, divine love: how to recognize spiritual love, awaken it, direct it and revel in it for the self, family & community. For forty years she's cultivated Bhakti yoga; is the Managing Editor for Bacopa Literary Review and blogs at Little Ways of Being.

Radha Dasi Cornia is a practitioner of Bhakti yoga who, along with her husband, serves a bhakti community in San Diego, California.

She is an attorney and a graduate of Harvard Law School. An activist at heart, she firmly believes that Bhakti yoga is the ultimate social revolution.

Becky Crigger has been teaching yoga, meditation, and spirituality for over ten years. She is currently enrolled in seminary at the School of Theology at the University of the South and is a postulant for Holy Orders in the Episcopal Church. Becky is dedicated to inter-religious dialogue and inter-spiritual practices, particularly the commonalities between Hindu philosophy and Christian mysticism.

Madhava Lata Devi Dasi has been practicing Bhakti Yoga for the past 36 years. Originally from Italy, she now lives in India, where -after a successful career- she continues to study and practice yoga. Her poems are about devotion and are published on her blog 'The Door Ajar to Vraja'. Lately some of her poems have been put to music.

Urmila Devi Dasi (Dr. Edith Best) is a practitioner of Bhakti yoga since 1973. Her books include *The Great Mantra for Mystic Meditation,* and she is an editor of *Back to Godhead,* an international spiritual journal. She and her husband have three grown married children and twelve grandchildren.

Rev. Doris Davis, now 75 years old, is an Interfaith Minister, spiritual activist, grandmother and freelance mystic. With her daughter, actress-filmmaker Viveka Davis, she completed a cross-country American walkabout in 2011, imagining a world where women are equally valued decision-makers -- in partnership with men -- worldwide.

Maira De La Cruz is a lover of music, art, literature, and nature. She follows the path of Bhakti yoga, a spiritual discipline meant to bring one to a state of pure love and devotion to the Supreme person, God, or Krishna. Her writings are solely inspired by Krishna and her experiences of self-realization.

Sarah Courtney Dean is a trans-gender woman and Druid Priestess living in the UK. She has been a poet for as long as she can remember and sees this as part of her role as a Druid Priestess and as a woman. This is a role of encouragement that others through her may find a voice.

Zola Dubnikova is a dance artist from Israel that has lived, performed and taught all over the world. She integrates mystical tradition with contemporary movements and holistic science to create a unique healing process. Zola devotes herself to using these healing modalities of dance to uplift women, mend their wounds and reconnect them to their divine source.

Shailie Dubois has a Psychology degree and practices *Intuitive Prayer Healing*. She integrates spirituality (Christianity, Bhakti yoga, Shamanism) with psychology and holistic energy techniques to help people recover the sacred within themselves. Her hands are forever busy, creating art, music or harvesting wild herbs.

Victoria Erickson is based in Austin, TX. Victoria leads creative writing workshops, is a holistic esthetician, massage therapist and Reiki practitioner. To find out more visit her website: victoriaerickson. com, or connect with her on Facebook @VLE1031 and Pinterest @ victorialynn756.

Sharon Gannon, co-creator of the Jivamukti Yoga method, is an animal rights activist and is the author of several books including *Simple Recipes For Joy, a vegan cookbook*. She writes a monthly essay, called the Focus of the Month, which can be read at: jivamuktiyoga.com.

Maru Garcia was born and raised in Mexico City. She has a degree in Nutrition and believes in Veganism as a walking statement of love. She is a strong advocate for animal welfare and their right to just be animals! Maru lives in Playa del Carmen with her 3 dogs, 2 birds and three cats.

Shahla Ghobadi (BE, MSc. PhD) is a university researcher, consultant, and, in her spare time, a poet. She considers Persian poetry, in particular Molavi (Rumi), instrumental in her research inspiration. Shahla is increasingly keen to reach out to poetry lovers around the world and to bringing different minds closer.

Jenn Grosso plays host to the dance of shadow and light, while smiling at the fleeting nature of it all. Embracing her inner sacred creativity, she focuses most of her time on reading, writing, painting/mixed media, yoga, meditation and picture taking. Connect with Jenn on her blog *Perils of the Living*, Facebook, Instagram and Twitter.

Salyna Gracie is a multi-media artist with a focus in dance, poetry and mixed-media collage. Her work explores movement, language and visual symbols that reveal the universal experience woven through the deeply personal terrain of inner truth. Evoking dreamscapes that are at once mystical and confessional, she raises questions of identity, memory, legacy and inheritance. Salyna is a lifelong student of the healing power of art as a deepening spiritual practice, and a window into her soul.

Jennifer Hawley-Zechlin is an amateur poet, lover of life, and professional dreamer and thinker. She lives with her partner of 25 years and their 17 year-old daughter in the mountains of Southern California. She reads far too many books, and experiments with painting and fluting in the middle of the night.

Jennieke Janaki was born in the Netherlands. While traveling the world for 12 years as a model she found her fulfillment in the practice of yoga. She founded 'Sharanam Yoga: Healing Through Surrender' in the Sivananda Lineage. Jennieke's poetry book is called *'Divine Sweetness: Love Aspirations"*. She lives every day as an opportunity to realize herself, and enjoys the path of finding the sanctuary within, where peace and joy abides for us, always.

Melissa June is from Windsor Ontario, Canada. She writes poetry that is metaphorical, poems of loneliness and poems of the dark side. She dreams of publishing a book of poetry one day. As a mother of three beautiful girls, she hopes to touch more upon children's rhymes in the future.

Krista Angelique Katrovas is an experienced Registered Yoga Teacher. She holds a BA in Dance and an MFA in Creative Writing. She has studied Yoga in India and calls Kalamazoo, Michigan home, where she owns Angelique's Boutique & Yoga, a business that strives to serve women and benefits the local women's shelter.

Aparna Khanolkar is a lover of life and beauty. She is fully engaged in life through the art and science of Ayurveda. Indian by birth, she lives in California with her two children and teaches workshops and classes on embracing the feminine and cultivating sovereignty as women. Website: AparnaKhanolkar.com.

Jacqui Lalita is an international dance instructor, performer, poet and storyteller passionate about helping people awaken to their hearts joy. Fusing Sufi whirling, Middle Eastern dance, and Romani gypsy dance, Jacqui leads sacred movement retreats in Bali, Turkey and Costa Rica where women have an opportunity to dive into intense dance study in the paradise of nature. She's authored two poetry books. Visit her website danceofthedivine.org.

Edith Lazenby has been writing poems since the age of nine. They keep her whole. She lives in Maryland with her two kitties and teaches yoga full time and writes and edits. You can find more of her at her blog at edieyoga.wordpress.com.

Sheri Lindner, Ph.D. is a clinical psychologist, poet and essayist whose writings have appeared in a variety of print and online journals and anthologies including: *Poetica, Jewish Currents, and The New York Times.* She was awarded First Prize in the 2nd Annual *Nassau County*

Poet Laureate Society Contest, and is currently the associate editor of *Jewish Women's Literary Annual.*

Solodad Maria is a Spiritual Midwife and healer of soul who believes in the gifts of the woman inside and the natural healer, sharing her love for humanity through her writings and energy work worldwide. www.spiritmidwifery.weebly.com

Mariann Martland is discovering a voice in her life through words, poetry, art, inspiration and healing. She is learning the difference between enforced silence in the despair of loneliness and chosen silence in the beauty of solitude; how silence can create both pain and peace. She is beginning to find her voice and share her truth.

Shiloh Sophia McCloud creates and teaches art as a spiritual discipline. She is the founder of Cosmic Cowgirls Ink, LLC: helping women develop their own creative potential. Shiloh has published over 5 books on creative expression, business as a visionary path and a book of poetry. Her classroom, as well as her art gallery featuring contemporary Symbolist paintings, is located in Healdsburg, California. Shilohsophiastudios.com

Mary McManus, MSW was diagnosed in 2006 with post polio syndrome. She did not take the diagnosis sitting down. She asked Spirit for guidance. Her pen became her divining rod for healing. Although her body was debilitated, for the first time, her Spirit flew free. Mary is a 2009 Boston Marathon finisher, the author of 5 books of inspirational poetry, and her memoir, "Coming Home: A Memoir of Healing, Hope and Possibility."

Maureen Kwiat Meshenberg relates to poetry as her passion and calling. She writes from the heart and with purpose. Her purpose is to touch others on their journey of life with her words of inspiration. She is currently working on publishing a book of poetry to be released November 2014. Her poetry can be found at heartscallingpoetry.com.

Kia Miller is one of the most well-known Kundalini teachers in the West. She has an ability to translate the subtle teachings of Kundalini Yoga in a highly accessible way. Kia's study of yoga began when she was 15. She is certified in both Hatha and Kundalini Yoga and teaches workshops, retreats and teacher trainings throughout the world.

Alexandra Moga is a writer and a yoga teacher living in New York. You can find more of her work at thepoetofmymind.com.

Jessica Mokrzycki lives in New England with her husband of 10 years and two small children. She writes about her search for a deeper understanding into the nature of reality and self on her blog: ascendingthehills.blogspot.com. She has found continued inspiration and spiritual direction from the Bhagavad Gita. Mindfulness and chanting the *maha mantra* on her *japa mala* have been the two most profound and transformative practices she has discovered on her journey towards understanding so far.

Ruth Calder Murphy (Arciemme) is a writer, artist, music teacher, wife and mother living in the UK. The author of several books, she's passionate about celebrating the uniqueness and diversity of people, questioning the unquestionable and discovering new perspectives on old wonders. Website: ruthcaldermurphy.com.

Tina Tadiya Nissinen is a *bhakti yogini* in the tradition of Sri Caitanya. She loves exploring spirituality, creativity and art. She has a Master's Degree in Theology & Religious Studies, and is currently studying Occupational Therapy and the use of creative methods in therapy. Tadiya lives in Finland. Read more of her writings on her blog: bhaktiblossoms.wordpress.com.

Yasmeen Amina Olya was raised in an environment full of creativity and is a Waldorf alumna. As an intuitive artist and musician she is deeply influenced by her spiritual path of Sufism, and love of nature. She currently lives on Vancouver Island, Canada where she frequently plays free open-air concerts. For more information visit her website www.yasmeensong.com.

Gwen Potts began her spiritual journey at 21 when she began reading spiritual articles, poetry and books of a spiritual nature. Now at 35 her poetry has become a vehicle of expression and always written from the depth of her soul. Her poems often well up as a yearning - truly written from the heart. Gwen lives in the UK.

Zoe Quiney is a writer, dreamer and believer in the power of words to inspire, help and heal. She currently resides in Sydney, where she writes, tries to be a good *yogini* and thanks her lucky stars for living by the beach. She writes a blog: follow-my-dreamer.blogspot.com.au which focuses on encouraging people to follow their dreams, not society's expectations.

Carolyn Riker is a poet and writer who lives in Seattle with her two children and cat. She currently writes for several journals and one of her essays was included in *Best of Rebelle Society.* Carolyn also works as a tutor and is publishing her first children's picture book.

Linda Yael Schiller, MSW, LICSW (www.lindayaelschiller.com) integrates body, mind and spirit as a psychotherapist, consultant, and trainer based in Watertown, MA. Linda teaches nationally on trauma and dissociation, energy therapies, dreamwork, group work, body/mind integration and spirituality in practice. She also writes poetry and a dream blog at Awakenyourdreams.com

Ruth Broyde Sharone is a passionate international speaker for peace-building, a filmmaker, journalist, and author. Ruth produced the prize-winning film, *God and Allah Need to Talk.* Her interfaith memoir, *Minefields & Miracles,* received endorsements from religious leaders, including H.H. the Dalai Lama. A poet and songwriter since she was 18, Ruth is currently composing a musical to promote interreligious harmony.

Beatrice Chemutai Sigei originally from Kenya, Africa, writes personal spiritual poetry and inspirational quotes on peace. She works as a fulltime psychiatric nurse and founder of a nonprofit organization called *Viola Safe Wells*, dedicated to making clean water accessible via wells and water safety education. She practices meditation.

Braja Sorensen is a writer, author, poet, photographer, *bhakti-yogini*, cook, cow lover, and strident *fashionista*. Originally from Australia, she now lives in India and published *Lost and Found In India* with Hay House International in 2013. Braja's award-winning poetry has been published in the UK and Australia. Connect with her at brajasorensen.com.

Camellia Stadts has been writing for many years but did not fall in love with poetry or creating poetry until recently after going through some of life's earthquakes. Poetry heals her heart and soul. She lives in Detroit, and has a son, daughter and grandson: her greatest joys.

Naomi Stone is a contemplative, a mystic, a pilgrim, a seeker, a writer, a poet, and a listener. She is an advocate of the freedom to live creatively, and a lover of nature who feels the sacramental presence of the Creator as a Beloved in each precious moment of life.

Savitri Talahatu is an interdisciplinary teacher, certified lifestyle coach and holistic health practitioner, doula and Reiki Master. She is passionate about inspiring women to make healthy lifestyle choices and find their own gateways to wholeness. Savitri facilitates workshops and Yoga teachers' training programs, and leads retreats in Canada and internationally.

Nirvani Teasley is a veteran Navy wife, mother of four grown children and two adorable granddaughters. She is a long time folk art painter and fabric artist. In the last two years, she has evolved from her lifelong passion for reading poetry, to writing it. She loves penning poems that emphasize the Divine Feminine.

Latika Teotia is a simple seeker who has journeyed forth to find self-realization through spreading the message of Love, Compassion and Kindness. She has a soft corner for special needs children and women who need their self-esteem raised. Connect with her through "Have Wings Will Fly", a Facebook page where she invites Self-Exploration and inspires others.

Rosemerry Wahtola Trommer's poetry has appeared in *O Magazine*, in back alleys, on *A Prairie Home Companion* and in her children's lunch boxes. Her most recent collection is "The Less I Hold." She is a parent educator for Parents as Teachers. Favorite one-word mantra: *Adjust*.

Margaret Vidale began writing poetry after retiring from teaching. Many of her early poems dealt with severe childhood abuse. Breaking over fifty years of silence was healing and liberating, and enabled Margaret to branch out into a wider range of subjects. Her thriving grandsons are daily inspirations.

Freya Watson's writing deals with common themes – love, sexuality and life – but with the broader perspective of one who carries a deep spirituality and a fascination with the cultures of the world. Her books include fiction and non-fiction, and are available both in print and e-book through Amazon.

Aisha Wolfe is a practitioner of spiritual transformation, a midwife to the void and phases of emergence. Her first poetry collection *Yoni Verse Burlesque* is available from emergingnow.co.uk. Unveiling Lilith, a journey of feminine empowerment will be published in 2014.

Jyoti (Rebecca) Yacobi lives in Toronto, Canada. She practices the yoga of Kashmiri Shaivism and is guided on this path by Swami Nirmalananda Saraswati. She works in the field of pediatric dentistry and also teaches yoga and meditation in the style of Svaroopa Yoga. Writing poetry has been a process of unfolding self-expression, of connecting to the source from which the voice originates.

Acknowledgements

This project was unexpectedly birthed from a period of conflict with my own voice. Aching to give my voice wings again, I sought to surround myself with the soaring voices of other women as inspiration. I chose poetry because, in my own life, poetry has rescued my voice, over and over again, more than anything else. It is this moment of doubt in my own voice that I acknowledge first, as it became the fuel for this whole idea: the dark night that allowed me to see the stars again. So I am very thankful for this struggle, as it surprised me by growing into a book!

Next, I extend my heartfelt gratitude to all the beautiful souls that participated in the *Journey of The Heart: Women's Spiritual Poetry* blog. It was they who gave me the idea for this book, and without whom this book would have never been possible. Their poems are like the juicy fruits on the branches of this endeavor, nourishing our hearts each time one of them was submitted to the blog. Of these women, ten played a special role in bringing forth this project through their consistent offerings of poetry and the enthusiastic energy that infused their participation: Carolyn Riker, Tadiya Dasi Nissinen, Ruth Calder Murphy, Jenn Grosso, Mary McManus, Noor-Malika Chishti, Edith Lazenby, Jessica Mokrzyckl, Maureen Kwiat Meshenberg and Krista Katrovas.

Many thanks to Braja Sorensen, my delightfully troublemaking friend and writing partner in Yoga in The Gita, who generously inundated the blog with her poetry, when the project was just in seed form. Braja's poem 'Fair Beauty' was the first to appear on 'Journey of The Heart'. It describes Radharani—the name given to the Divine Feminine in the Bhakti Yoga tradition—on whose Holy Day in the fall of 2012, the blog upon which this book is based, was first launched.

My heartfelt gratitude and respect to my inspired friend Pranada Comtois, who over cups of tea, and through long walks in the woods, shared valuable insights with me about writing as a spiritual process, and the power of the Divine Feminine voice within us all. Her enthusiasm for engaging poetry as a means of cultivating self-realization, resonated deeply with my own life experience, and added to the inspirations behind this project. Since my adolescence, Pranada has been a cheerleader of my voice, and that of all women, ever intent on helping us believe in ourselves.

I am especially appreciative of my dearest friend and spiritual sister, Vrinda Aguilera, who spent hours and hours with me over the course of the last couple of years, exploring and analyzing, dissecting and intellectualizing the creative process with me, and its endlessly mysterious ways. Most importantly, she lovingly helped me identify and overcome obstacles preventing me from expressing my own voice, and through her healing words, managed to fill my sails with wind whenever I began to stagnate.

These acknowledgements of the women in my life, who helped me connect in very powerful ways to the healing potency in a poem, would not be complete with out mentioning my beloved friend, Carmela Hapach, who once described my voice to me as a bird in a cage that desperately needed freeing. It was Carmela's poetry that first began rattling at my cage, over fifteen years ago, when we'd stay up late into the night reading poems and serving as each other's muses.

I'd also like to extend my love and gratitude to my beloved sister, Lisa, in whose eyes I could always do anything I set my heart on: a person who has believed in the value of my words ever since we were little girls. And to my beautiful, spiritual sisters, Jahnavi Briant, Ladali Cabezas, Atmesvari Haldhar and Subhadra Sluder Hemphill, in whose loving friendships I exercised my voice over the decades.

Thank you to my two patient sons, Gopal and Nrisimha, who were good sports about taking over laundry and meal preparation while their mother worked on this manuscript.

A very special and loving appreciation goes to my dear mother, Lynda Grace Patrick Vargas, who not only shared her love of poetry with me at a very young age, but also served as a highly skilled and experienced editor, offering her tireless proofreading to the manuscript at various phases of completion. I am greatly indebted to her, and to my father, Jorge A. Vargas, for their continued encouragement and support of this book. It was my father who printed my first poetry book for me when I was eighteen, always encouraging me to publish my voice. I will never forget the day, when—at eleven years old—I approached him with a heavy heart, discouraged by the suffering around the world, and desperate to help alleviate it in whichever way I could. And my father told me one thing: "Write!", which he continues to do to this day.

To my heart's life partner, Graham M. Schweig, I offer my deepest gratitude and love, for it was he who insisted that my voice was most precious, even long after its wings had been clipped. Graham helped me find the courage to fly again.

CPSIA information can be obtained at www.ICGtesting.com
Printed in the USA
LVOW06s0915080814

398043LV00005B/7/P

9 781452 517827